GOING BACK TO FIND
THE WAY
FORWARD

Trump, A Great Awakening, and The Refounding of America

MIKE D'VIRGILIO

SILVERSMITH
PRESS

Published by Silversmith Press—Houston, Texas
www.silversmithpress.com

ISBN 978-1-961093-46-1 (Softcover Book)
ISBN 978-1-961093-47-8 (eBook)

To my mother, Geline,
who raised me to be a semi-normal person
in a crazy Italian family.

CONTENTS

INTRODUCTION

When Donald Trump started his descent down the escalator at Trump Tower on June 16, 2015, there was a rip in the space-time continuum. I'm not sure what that means, but in God's providence something clearly remarkable happened that day. This is so much bigger than Donald Trump, but it was the visceral response to Trump that triggered everything, and nothing remotely like it has happened in modern American political history. I qualify this with modern because most Americans are unaware of how contentious American politics was in the eighteenth and nineteenth centuries. This book is basically my red-pill journey, a testimony if you will, starting when Donald Trump came down that escalator—and completely unbeknownst to me—slowly started a change in my perspective about almost everything. The same is happening for multitudes of Americans, and in that lies our great opportunity. It is also about finding our way back to first principles so we can with wisdom make our way forward to give to future generations all the blessings America's founders gave to us.

Many people talk about how Trump exposed the "Fake News Media" and the so-called deep state, among other things. Being a developer and builder, Trump turned out to be the guy who pulled the siding off the house revealing teaming throngs of termites underneath. God, in his providence, used the most unlikely person in Donald J. Trump, billionaire real estate developer and reality TV star, to reveal the spiritual darkness at the heart of American cultural and political life. God always seems to use unlikely people, as a read through redemptive history in the Bible makes abundantly clear. This applies not only to the redemptive history revealed in Scripture, but to *all* history, which is ultimately redemptive. We will explore what this means from my perspective in the pages to come.

It is odd for me to think of Trump in this way because for me when he came down that escalator it was a non-event. To say the least, I was *not* a fan. I thought he was every stereotype his enemies claimed: a narcissistic, shallow, materialist, blowhard womanizer (prior to that most of those enemies loved him, and took his money), and as an Evangelical Christian I would *never* consider supporting him. I was sure his campaign was a joke, a self-serving publicity stunt. Even as a bit of a news junkie, I was only vaguely aware this stunt even happened because the space-time continuum seemed perfectly safe. When I learned he was running for president, I yawned. That, I was sure, would *never* happen. I remember vividly telling my wife in October, Donald Trump will *never* be president. The very idea seemed preposterous. I guess I'm not as tuned into God's providence as I like to think I am, but alas, thankfully, God's doing is often as unpredictable as it appears mysterious.

As the Republican primary heated up in 2016 and the debates got under way, I began to take a more serious look at Trump. One reason my mind started opening to him was how over the top his critics were. I thought, no man can possibly be *that* bad. I also noticed his children were relatively well-adjusted adults who seemed to sincerely love and admire their father. Narcissistic psychopaths can't pull that off. Another reason was reading and listening to people I respected take his ideas and positions seriously. Some positions were not your typical conservative boilerplate, which hadn't done much to change anything in a conservative direction culturally or politically in the previous several decades. Living in Illinois at that time, I was hesitant to vote for Trump in the June primary, almost feeling guilty I was even considering it. It took my mother-in-law to convince me to vote for Trump over Cruz, and reluctantly I did. What I didn't realize at the time is how God was using this man to change the orientation of my worldview in a variety of ways I could never have imagined. In the overused word of Vizzini in *The Princess Bride*, it was "inconceivable!"

Having a passion for apologetics, I can't help seeing what's been happening as God's revelation of Himself in history and His providential ordaining of all things toward His glorious ends. Therefore, I see this book as a work of apologetics, but it's a different kind of apologetics animal. There are a variety of ways of defending the Christian faith. Normally evidence of various kinds is amassed, historical, philosophical, textual, etc., and arguments are made and conclusions drawn. My defense, by contrast, assumes Christianity is true, and evidence for it is discovered as God works throughout history to achieve what Jesus commanded us to pray, "Thy kingdom come, thy will be done on earth as it is in heaven." I'm unlikely to *prove* this to anyone who doesn't already believe it or is not open to the idea, but that's not my goal. I always appreciate it when Dennis Prager says his objective isn't necessarily agreement, but clarity. I hope my argument and ideas are clear and are at least worthy of consideration for those who don't share my theological and philosophical assumptions. Most importantly, I want them to consider my conclusions, even if they don't take them to the metaphysical ends I do.

This book is also a labor of education. I had no idea where this book was going when I started thinking about it, but it has been an amazing educational experience for me. I hope it can also be something like that for those who read it.

We are obviously in a momentous and consequential moment in the history of the world. I had no idea when I started writing that my argument would turn out to be so counterintuitive: things are looking good even though they're often looking really, really bad. In fact, things have to often get really bad before they start to get really good, before the reveal can happen. Yoram Hazony understands this:

> [T]he sudden rise of the new Marxists presents an opportunity for a conservative revival unlike any we have seen in our lifetimes. To be sure, we are witnessing a spectacular and horrifying historical event. The potential for tragedy is obviously very great. But the extremity of this event can permit a process of rethinking that had been impossible until now. Many will now find that they are ready for the rediscovery that I have described: the rediscovery of a conservative life.[1]

He is right. Unfortunately, it is the *necessity* of the horribleness we're experiencing that presents the opportunity to make fundamental changes toward a re-founding of America. Even though he is an observant conservative Jew, Hazony sees the necessity of a re-flourishing of Christianity in Western culture if it is to survive. For that to happen, Christians are going to have to cooperate and act. Readers will learn why Christianity is central to this re-flourishing, so we can more effectively address the how. We must also cooperate with non-Christians because America belongs to all of us. While I write as an American largely to an American context, the message is universal because Christianity is universal.

As for those who don't share my Christian convictions or biblical assumptions, my hope for them is clarity as well. I am seeking to disabuse them of the common secular notion—that Christianity is narrow minded, intolerant, and inherently tyrannical, and that Christian rule in a nation or culture is bad for liberty and against the basic political principles we've come to take for granted in the West. As we'll see, quite the contrary is true. Liberty and these principles are largely a product of Christianity! Without Christianity there is no such idea as the West, no rule of law or political liberalism, no such thing as pluralism and real religious liberty, no free speech, no America! Not to mention there is no science, capitalism and prosperity, hospitals and healthcare, universal education, and literacy. They will learn how indebted we are for these things to Jesus of Nazareth, whose disciples declared him to be the Christ, the long-awaited Jewish Messiah, who they claim rose from the dead, ascended to heaven, and sent his Holy Spirit to make all this happen![2]

Finally, we are all in this together, Christians and non-Christians alike. We battle against the ever-present human temptation toward Babel, of man thinking he can be as God. It is the God revealed to us in creation, Scripture, and Christ against whom the globalists wage war. I believe the exposing of this enemy in our tumultuous times reveals that we are in midst of another Great Awakening. People see this awakening from a variety of perspectives and time will tell its true nature, but many agree truth is being revealed; reality is punching back because it can only be mocked for so long. Come with me in these pages to see one Christian's take on this world transforming time in which we live.

RED PILLS AND THE NEXT GREAT AWAKENING

It seems like I must have taken a time-release red pill sometime after Donald Trump announced his run for president in 2015. Although technically you choose to take it, when you realize you've been "red-pilled" as we've come to use it, you understand it's really not a choice. It's something that happens when you least expect it, and I never expected what's been happening to me since Trump came down the escalator at Trump Tower to announce his run for the presidency in June of 2015.

The reason the red-pill metaphor works and has become so widely used is because of the 1991 film, *The Matrix*, from which we take the concept. The hero, Neo, played by Keanu Reeves, is given a choice by Morpheus, Laurence Fishburne, of a red or a blue pill. The scene captures why we talk so much about these red pills.

> MORPHEUS: It's that feeling you have had all your life. That feeling that something was wrong with the world. You don't know what it is but it's there, like a splinter in your mind, driving you mad, driving you to me. But what is it? The Matrix is everywhere, it's all around us, here even in this room. You can see it out

your window, or on your television. You feel it when you go to work or go to church or pay your taxes. It is the world that has been pulled over your eyes to blind you from the truth.

NEO: What truth?

MORPHEUS: That you are a slave, Neo. That you, like everyone else, was born into bondage... kept inside a prison that you cannot smell, taste, or touch. A prison for your mind. Unfortunately, no one can be told what the Matrix is. You have to see it for yourself.

NEO: How?

MORPHEUS: Hold out your hands. (He holds a red and a blue pill.) This is your last chance. After this, there is no going back. You take the blue pill and the story ends. You wake in your bed, and you believe whatever you want to believe. You take the red pill, and you stay in Wonderland, and I show you how deep the rabbit-hole goes. Remember that all I am offering is the truth. Nothing more.

Funny how nobody admits being "blue pilled." Unfortunately, most people are, but that's changing.

"The Matrix is everywhere" perfectly captures the secular, progressive worldview that completely dominates all organs of cultural and political power in the West, the elites, and the ruling class. The laundry list is well-known by now: media, the entertainment industry, education (all so called public schools, save charter classical schools, and practically all colleges and universities), big business, professional and college sports, the legal profession, and of course, government at every level. In the pages to come I will explore this worldview and how antithetical it is to everything Christian and anything that leads to a healthy functioning and flourishing civilization. The evidence is everywhere for those with eyes to see, red pill or not.

The secular, progressive religion (faith commitment) of Western elites can be understood in sociological terms as a plausibility structure, a helpful concept to understand how this Matrix works. Something plausible *seems* real to us, whether it is or not. Adding the word "structure" means there is a reality-generating societal building we inhabit, and when we're in it, everything *seems* real to us, *seems* true, *seems* like that's just the way things are—until they're not. Then we begin to question the seeming realness of these things, and thus we've been red-pilled. What was once plausible to us, seemed real, concrete, the nature of things, now loses its plausibility. Suddenly, we begin to question what until only recently we took for granted as "the way things are."

After Donald Trump won the Republican nomination, I started questioning things I had taken for granted most of my life. For many like me, he proved to be a walking red pill. As the irrationality and lying of those infected with Trump Derangement Syndrome (TDS) became more apparent in the ensuing years, my questioning became more significant. A so-called pandemic, the 2020 stolen election, and the January 6 "insurrection" took TNT to what was left of my pre-Trump plausibility structure. I was now questioning everything. I think I was even in danger of becoming a certified "conspiracy theorist;" the fever swamps weren't looking so hot, sweaty, and diseased anymore. Truth was being revealed to me like a shipwreck as the water recedes and you can finally see the whole outline of the ship. God was lowering the waters.

MY RED PILL JOURNEY

For me, the "splinter in my mind," the thing driving me mad, to my metaphorical Morpheus, was the political status quo in America for the last 50 years. In 1978 as a freshman in college I embraced a type of born-again Christianity, what we refer to today generally as Evangelical. I discovered the works of Francis Schaeffer and because of him after Reagan was elected realized I was a conservative. I subscribed to *National Review* magazine and started reading the *Wall Street Journal* editorial page (both of which unfortunately got TDS). Thus began my broad political and cultural education.

For more than two decades, I never realized there was something seriously wrong with "the establishment," including Republicans and those who call themselves conservatives. In fact, it was because of Republicans, and what appeared to me their continual failure, that I began to feel the "splinter in my mind." I thought, like most conservatives, that just voting in the right politicians, those who said the right things, would bring real change. Yet, nothing ever changed. Government continued getting bigger, more powerful, and more intrusive in our lives, and culture growing ever more coarse and anti-Christian.

One of the first breaking points preparing me for my awakening was the 2006 mid-term elections. The Republicans got shellacked. I was despondent as I realized my problem was thinking politics alone could solve our cultural and societal problems. Clearly *that* wasn't working. I discovered something the late Andrew Breitbart said, that *politics is downstream from culture*. For decades conservatives had tried to change the culture and our society via politics all but ignoring culture, other than complaining about it.

I decided I was going to do something about this, and in the next few years started a non-profit I initially called The Culture Project. My objective was to encourage more conservatives and Christians to get involved in what I called the professions of cultural influence; media, entertainment, education, etc. I found some guys who agreed with me, we started writing for a website, and did some events. In the summer of 2009, I was in New York City for a business trip, and was able to get a meeting with the president of the Hudson Institute, the late Herb London. I was going on in my typically demonstrative fashion about the importance of culture and must have said some things about politics not being so very important. Herb, a wise man said, "Well, politics is the distribution of power, so it is very important." I wouldn't call it a rebuke, but it got my attention.

Looking back, I realize I was in the middle of my continuing education in developing a political philosophy. I had never thought about having a coherent philosophy of politics before I started thinking about writing this book. I've since realized I should have a distinctly Christian understanding about how we as the American people ought to govern ourselves, as well as how Christianity applies to nation states in general.

Then, Trump came down the escalator.

After almost 35 years of political, cultural, and theological education, it was time to earn my master's degree in political philosophy from a biblical perspective, only without the school part. I will explore this in detail as the book unfolds because my red pill experiences have caused me to take a new look at how my Christian worldview affects my understanding of America and Christian Western civilization as it relates to the kingdom of God.

To do that I will need to connect the red-pill period we've been living through to the gospel, the church, and the advance of God's kingdom. I imagine many Christians would not see the mess we've been going through *as ultimately evangelical*, but I've come to see it that way. My passion in life is the proclamation of the gospel, and the exaltation of the risen Jesus, the long-awaited Jewish Messiah and Savior of the world. I know it will be "controversial" to argue that Donald Trump has been used by God to further the gospel and God's kingdom, but you'll have to bear with me to see if I make the case.

As Christians, though, there is only one way to look at history, as well as history as it unfolds before our eyes. It's about the coming of God's kingdom (as Jesus says, "Thy will be done on earth as it is in heaven"), and the extension of Christ's church throughout the world, against which the gates of hell shall not prevail. John the Baptist paved the way for the coming of the Messiah with, "Repent, for the kingdom of heaven is near," and after Jesus was tempted by Satan in the wilderness, He began His earthly ministry repeating John's words verbatim. His ministry, life, death, and resurrection were to bring the kingdom of God, or "the kingdom of the heavens" to earth. We'll see how this has been accomplished throughout history and is being done in our day.

HOW GOD USED A "PANDEMIC" AND A STOLEN ELECTION TO OPEN MY EYES

To further explore the premise of this book, I will share a bit more of my journey, and why I've given it such deep spiritual import. As of late January 2020, I was still watching Fox News, and one day noticed a scene at an airport of Chinese people not being allowed into the US. I heard it had something to do with a virus, and I thought, *whatever it is, it's trivial, part of another passing news cycle going nowhere.* Oh boy, was I wrong!

As things developed and Trump declared Covid an emergency, I didn't think much about it. Democrats mocked Trump's concern, calling him a xenophobe, common to their list of Trump epithets. Nancy Pelosi even said that we should find a Chinese person to hug on Chinese New Year which fell on February 1 of that year. Then in March, they did a 180 degree turn. It was as if a 40-million-watt light bulb went off in the heads of the collective left, *We can use this "pandemic" against Trump!* Suddenly, Covid was akin to the bubonic plague, the black death that wiped out some 20 million people, or approximately 40% of the population of Europe in the mid fourteenth century. I realized someone, likely several someones, somewhere, with enough pull, decided Covid could be used to destroy Trump.

Depending on where one comes down on the "conspiracy continuum," this was either mere political theater, Democrats and the media cynically using "public health" to destroy their political opponents, or a worldwide cabal of global elites who wanted to de-populate the earth because of the green agenda. Naomi Wolf calls it "pandemic totalitarianism" and I'm inclined to agree. I'm sure some involved thought the virus was a real threat and were well-intentioned, however nothing about the response to Covid passed the smell test.

With the help of my cousin, a doctor, I started questioning everything about modern medicine, what I now call the medical-industrial complex, Big Pharma, so-called "experts," everything. Public health became an oxymoron to me. Apart from political and medical considerations, Covid was the secular-progressive worldview on steroids, and there are many reasons why. Understood in the most benign way possible, the Covid response was the culmination of the progressive rule by "experts" that began to dominate Western culture at the turn of the twentieth century. I decided to study the history of modern medicine. The more I learned, the more I realized I'd been indoctrinated into discounting God's amazing immune system to heal the body, in favor of a science-medicine first approach. I now began to see my health in light of the kingdom of God.

The human body, its immune system, and the earth are meant to sustain us; this was now to me part of God's revelation in creation (Rom. 1:20). I've always known that, but this was different. All this knowledge we've been given is for the glory of God and His kingdom come on earth. When Jesus healed people during His ministry it wasn't merely a metaphor for spiritual healing, which it clearly was. It was also a metaphor for the coming of His kingdom in physical self-healing and medicine when it's appropriate. Christians, especially we Protestant Evangelical Christians, tend to over spiritualize and moralize everything. We think God's kingdom coming is primarily about the saved going to heaven and everyone being more moral, better people, nicer, more loving, less conflict, less anger, less sexual dysfunction, and so on. It is that, but it's so much more.

My health epiphany was amazing and exciting, but it was also distressing. I had been indoctrinated to see things a certain way all my life, in this case medicine and health. I never thought to question any of it. I'd been skeptical of the pronouncements of "experts" and their "studies" for a long time, but never questioned the fundamental paradigm of how medicine and our healthcare system were supposed to work. Suddenly, watching the medical establishment being used for blatant political purposes was heartbreaking and frustrating. For example, Trump and some Republicans had been warning about mail-in voting for a while, which was being pushed by Democrats because of Covid; however, nothing would prepare me and millions of others for what happened on November 3, and the morning of November 4, 2020. I'm not interested in adjudicating Covid or the election, only in pointing out how this big, huge, red pill tasted bitter, but has proved sweeter than I could have imagined at the time.

STEVE BANNON AND HIS WAR ROOM POSSE COME TO THE RESCUE

It could not have been more obvious that the election was compromised. I'm convinced God in His providence allowed this to happen in order to red pill millions of Americans who previously saw politics as fundamentally honest and above board. In 2016, the elite were convinced Trump had no chance, so they didn't orchestrate a steal. His election broke the left and their RINO (Republican in Name Only) enablers, or as Bannon calls them, the controlled opposition. In 2020, Trump would simply not be allowed to win, period. They didn't care who knew or how obvious it was. They were convinced that after the steal, they could control "the narrative," and would silence or shame anyone who dared question the results. That hasn't worked any better on the election than it did on Covid.

Not long after the election I found Steve Bannon's *War Room*. I didn't know much about Bannon at the time, but little did I know how important he would become to my life and so many others' as well. I often say that Bannon got me out of the fetal position, and to mix metaphors, talked me off the ledge. He has no time for thumb suckers, and I was feeling pretty hopeless at the time. What I love about Bannon is his affirmation of our agency, meaning we are responsible for our lives and can change things. This is simple, but profound, a function of our being made in God's image. We often forget that we do have agency, that we're not cogs in a big machine as the progressive secular left wants us to believe, and as we too often see ourselves. Since the election, I've gotten an almost daily dose of Bannon's war cry of our agency in his mantra of "action, action, action!"

All I could think of at the time, however, was *they got away with it!* If Covid led to a health epiphany, the stolen election led to my political epiphany. That is why I'm writing this book. The epiphany is that the kingdom of God also advances politically, but more on that to come.

Then the January 6, 2021 "insurrection" happened, and that was the straw that broke the proverbial camel's back. The more I learned about that day, the more video I watched, the more apparent to me it was a setup to destroy the political opponents of the new, and I am convinced, fraudulent administration. It was the beginning of my journey down the rabbit-hole of the security state's corruption, led by the Department of Justice and FBI. I never realized just how corrupt our government, and the media, was until witnessing the full-scale war against Donald Trump. I could pick many examples, but several years of "Trump-Russia collusion" must top the list of lies, since conclusively proved false by the Durham Report. Congressman Devin Nunes said, "The scale of the abuse was astounding."[1] Speaking of his father, Donald Trump, Jr. said, "It was all a PR stunt...They wanted to destroy him and his family. As an American I still couldn't fathom in my mind they could be so corrupt and malicious. If they can do it to me, to the president, to Flynn, who won't they destroy to push their political will?"[2] Exactly. Little did we know at the time, although we should have, that the left would never stop, couldn't stop, until Trump was destroyed and no longer a threat to the ruling elite's grift. Now it's multiple indictments, which only seem to make Trump more sympathetic and popular.

The Democrats, media, and even many Republicans, have been lying about President Trump since he came down the escalator, but as I said in the introduction, this is about much more than Donald Trump. I look at all this, as I do everything, in light of God's providence.

Nothing happens by accident. History is not an inexorable process *a la Hegel*, predetermined toward some inevitable end. God is in control of all things toward His perfect end, as Scripture makes abundantly clear. God's providence allowed America's improbable founding to happen, and it will be His providence that allows its improbable re-founding.

EXAMPLES OF THE RED PILLING OF AMERICA AND WESTERN CULTURE

This awakening started happening well before Trump. For many on the left, Soviet Communism was a big red pill in the twentieth century. One-time communists like Whittaker Chambers, Irving Kristol, Norman Podhoretz and his wife Midge Decter, David Horowitz, and many others, became liberals because communism wasn't living up to the hype. Kristol referred to this as being "mugged by reality."

In the twenty-first century, the process of the current awakening arguably started with the election of the most radical leftist to attain the American presidency, Barack Obama. Five days before the 2008 election he clearly stated his radical, revolutionary goals, "We are five days away from fundamentally transforming the United States of America." Most Americans didn't pay attention to these breathtaking words. Few had any idea what he meant or took his statement seriously; all they could see was his skin color, big smile, smooth talk, and platitudes. The evidence for the fundamental nature of this change can be seen not just in his progressive policies, but in the corresponding direction of the media-industrial complex. The media has always had a Democrat-left bias, but since Edward R. Murrow in the 1950s, there was always the pretense of objectivity. With Obama, that completely went out the window. Leftist groupthink also made its way out of academia into the culture via the media.

In the Spring 2020 journal *Academic Questions*, Dr. David Rozado did a word frequency usage study on *New York Times* articles written between 1970 and the end of 2018.[3] He was looking for progressive/Marxist buzzwords used by groups with an ideological agenda. He discovered in 2010 and the years following such words and phrases had exploded in frequency. There are numerous charts in the article graphically displaying the jump in terms such as climate change, sexism, patriarchy, transphobia, homophobia, white supremacy, and so on. Apparently, all these things became such critically important issues around 2010 that America's "paper of record" found it necessary to endlessly report upon them. In fact, they were doing what the left always does, driving "the narrative," but in this case it went into overdrive. Joseph Goebbels would have been impressed.

If the media bias in the Obama Era was becoming undeniable, it went full-on steroids when Trump came on the scene. Because of Trump, the term "Fake News" stuck, but fake doesn't begin to describe the blatant lying that became media stock in trade. Everything started to be seen through the lens of hurting Trump or not, which was fine for most liberals because, well, Trump. But for many honest liberals who are not leftists, who still believed in and cared about truth, this move by their media buddies, normal allies, was raising red flags. Woke culture, long tyrannical on college campuses, was taking over newsrooms and corporate board rooms. Covid and the 2020 election season, with the silencing of free speech and big tech de-platforming, made the globalist totalitarian nature of the threat to Western civilization undeniable to a growing number of liberals.

Many are well-known, but I will end this chapter with the incredible red pill experience of Naomi Wolf. I witnessed her transformation in real time on Steve Bannon's *War Room* as he consistently interviewed her starting in early 2021. A secular Jewish liberal feminist author who had been an articulate enemy of all things conservative for decades, she was the last person I could imagine becoming a regular on *War Room*. She is one of those honest liberals referenced above who believes truth is more important than "the narrative" or a political agenda. One of the things liberals are supposed to care about is liberty, and fundamental to their worldview is a distrust of government and corporate power. This all got turned on its head with Obama, and God used Trump to reveal who the true liberals are.

What amazed me was her spiritual transformation. In early 2022 she wrote a piece titled, "Is it Time for Intellectuals to Talk about God?" Then I saw her interviewed by Tal Bachman on Rumble, and I was stunned by the reason for her transformation: evil. In her book, *The Bodies of Others: The New Authoritarians, COVID-19 and The War Against the Human*, she writes about a medical freedom activist. She asked him how he handled the attacks and social ostracism. He replied with Ephesians 6:12: "For our struggle is not against flesh and blood, but against the rulers, against the authorities, against the powers of this dark world and against the spiritual forces of evil in the heavenly realms." As things went on, this began to make sense to her:

> After many years of thinking that my spiritual life was not that important, I started to pray again. I'd once have thought that was very personal, almost embarrassingly so, and thus it was not something I should mention in public. But now, at a gathering in the woods with the health-freedom community, I told the group that I was now willing to speak about God publicly. Why? Because I had looked at what had descended on us from every angle, using my normal critical training yet found that it was so elaborate in its construction and so cruel, with an almost superhuman flamboyant, baroque imagination made from the essence of cruelty itself, that I could not conceive that it had been accomplished by mere humans working on the bumbling human level in the dumb political space.
>
> In the magnitude of the evil around us; in its awe-inspiring level of darkness and inhumanity; in the policies aimed at killing children's joy, restricting their breath, speech, and laughter; at killing ties between families and extended families; at killing churches and synagogues and mosques; and from the highest levels, from the president's own bully pulpit, demanding people to collude in excluding, rejecting, dismissing, shunning, hating their neighbors and

loved ones and friends: in all of this the presence of such rampant, elemental evil I felt a darkness beyond anything human. I don't think humans are smart or powerful enough to have come up with this horror all alone.

So, I told the group in the woods that the very impressiveness of evil all around us in all of its awful majesty was leading me to believe in a newly literal and immediate way the presence, the possibility, the necessity of a countervailing force—God.

As a classical liberal writer in a post-war world that was a huge leap for me to take—and to say out loud.[4]

As far as I know she has not made it all the way to Jesus, but I am praying for her. Whatever the case, we can say with certainty, she is much closer to her Messiah now because of Covid.

Many other things have happened since 2015 to convince me God is working through His sovereign control of all things to further His kingdom on earth and the advancement of the gospel. In the Matrix, Morpheus said: "Remember that all I am offering is the truth. Nothing more." To that we turn next.

CHAPTER 2

THE DIVIDING LINE IN WESTERN CULTURE: THE TRUTH

As with anything else in movements of cultures and societies, it's a complicated business. What we know as left and right in America, liberalism and conservatism as political and cultural constructs, have been around in America since after World War II. Many date the rise of modern conservatism to the publication of William F. Buckley's *God and Man at Yale* in 1951, and his founding of *National Review* Magazine in 1955. The difference between left and right until 2008 was significant, but the two sides at least lived on the same planet. When Obama came to power, the Democrats embraced a man of the radical left, a "community organizer" who believed America needed fundamental transformation. The vision of Obama and the left indicated a profound shift in American politics and culture related to the necessary existence of truth. By 2020 that shift had become a gulf wider than the Grand Canyon.

THIRD WAYISM AND THE DECEIT OF MORAL EQUIVALENCE

I first need to address those who muddy the cultural waters making it hard to even tell if there is a line between left and right, let alone where or what it is. As an example, I will regrettably use someone who was significantly influential in my theological and apologetics development, the late Tim Keller. Third Wayism is a kind of moral equivalence between the two, a third way, and Keller believed it. I will use a quote from a *World Magazine* article he wrote from early 2022 titled, "Handling a hostile culture: Assessing how the Church is responding to shifting cultural pressures":

> [T]he culture is definitely more polarized than it ever has been, and I've never seen the kind of conflicts in churches in the past that we see today. In virtually every church there is a smaller or larger body of Christians who have been radicalized to the Left or to the Right by extremely effective and completely immersive internet and social media loops, newsfeeds, and communities. People are bombarded 12 hours a day with pieces that present a particular political point of view, and the main way it seeks to persuade is not through argument but through outrage. People are being formed by this immersive form of public discourse—far more than they are being formed by the Church.

It is extremely disappointing that he really believed this. The phrase, "radicalized to the Left or to the Right," is not only unjustified, but a distortion of our political and cultural moment. There is simply no comparison between the two because there is no "radical right." It all turns on how one defines "radical," and Keller never bothers to do that. In the summer of 2020, the truly "radical" left in the form of BLM and Antifa, with the tacit encouragement of Democrats and their media allies, rioted in cities throughout the country and the media called them "mostly peaceful protests." There were billions of dollars of damage, and many lives lost. There is nothing comparable on the right. The so-called "insurrection" of January 6, 2021 was an FBI setup meant to demonize and silence Trump supporters and the entire MAGA movement.

Further, his point about what are in effect political feedback loops is nonsense. The secular left dominates all the organs of cultural influence, has the biggest megaphones, and their messaging cannot be escaped. They own all major media, practically all education, entertainment, and social media. People don't have to do anything to be programmed in leftist groupthink. On the contrary if you want alternative conservative views you have to search for them.

Andrew T. Walker had this to say about this Evangelical threading the needle:

> Third-wayism in politics is a form of political Gnosticism as it assumes that there is a platonic ideal to politics that does not require engaging the kingdoms of the world as what they fundamentally are: worldly, temporal, & creational ordinances designed for proximate justice.[1]

To think anyone can be apolitical in our day, least of all ministers of the gospel, is naïve at best, and delusional at worst. I've heard it said, you may not be into politics, but politics is into you, as the last several years make very clear. For the woke left, there is nothing beyond politics, which is why politics cannot be ignored or avoided. We'll explore what politics is and why Christians need to be involved in it in a later chapter, but we live in a definitional time and an existential crisis for America. The very existence of America bearing any relationship to our founding is on the line. Politicians and ministers who don't get the nature of the war we're engaged in, and it is a spiritual war between good and evil, do not understand, in Jesus' words, "the signs of the times."

The dividing line I'm talking about isn't a simple breakdown between Christians and non-Christians. As third wayism suggests, plenty of Christians don't recognize the signs of the times in which we live. I'm specifically focusing, however, on those who prior to Trump would likely be considered secular and irreligious, and certainly not practicing Christians. Such people would not in normal times be attracted to Christianity but have become, by their belief in and commitment to truth, far closer to the kingdom of God and Christianity than they would have been otherwise. They are also allies in our battle to save America and re-establish Christian Western civilization, and we will explore why.

"WHAT IS TRUTH?"

When Pilate asks Jesus this cynical question, we can file it under *the more things change, the more they stay the same.* Skepticism, doubt whether we can know what is true, is nothing new. The context of Pilate's interrogation of Jesus (John 18) is instructive for our dividing line discussion. Pilate asked Jesus if He is the king of the Jews, and Jesus answered that His kingdom was not of this world. Pilate correctly infers Jesus is saying He is a king and asks if He is. Jesus answers, "You say that I am a king. In fact, the reason I was born and came into the world is to testify to the truth. Everyone who is of the truth listens to my voice."

Then Pilate asks this famous question, and Jesus doesn't answer because he would have had to say, *I am!* (John 14:6)

Because truth is ultimately ground in a person; its metaphysical, spiritual, and ultimately personal dimension cannot be escaped. Truth is more profound than mere facts about things, however it is that and it is the nature of things that point back to the one who is Truth.

C.S. Lewis said, "Truth is always *about* something, but reality is *about which* truth is."[2] There is a God-ordained structure to reality, both in the obvious physical sense science reveals, but also in the moral sense. If we do not live in accordance with this structure, physically or morally, we suffer. Truth rooted in the divine is infinitely profound, but it is also infinitely practical and necessary for life in a fallen world full of lies. It will be helpful to go back to the beginning of the revelation of truth, and its antithesis, lies. And I mean back to the *very* beginning to see how lies were introduced into God's perfectly good, created world.

In Genesis 1, God using the power of His word, "said" eight times "let there be," and there was. Everything came into being. He added six times that "it was good," and added in a perfect biblical seven, "God saw all that He had made, and it was very good." The state of very good didn't last long though, and corruption entered the world through the lies of the accuser Satan in the form of a serpent. The devil's an ingenious liar and his tempting of Eve shows his diabolical talent well.

Adam had warned Eve about eating from the tree of the knowledge of good and evil, but we see in Genesis 3 it wasn't enough: Now the serpent was more crafty than any of the wild animals the Lord God had made. He said to the woman, "Did God really say, 'You must not eat from any tree in the garden'?"

His lie was so blatantly false, Eve didn't fall for it, but he accomplished his goal, questioning the character of God.

> ² The woman said to the serpent, "We may eat fruit from the trees in the garden, ³ but God did say, 'You must not eat fruit from the tree that is in the middle of the garden, and you must not touch it, or you will die.'"

God didn't say anything about touching it, but Satan came back with a lie that directly contradicted God's command.

> ⁴ "You will not certainly die," the serpent said to the woman. ⁵ "For God knows that when you eat from it your eyes will be opened, and you will be like God, knowing good and evil."

The rest, as they say, is history; a history that attests to the misery, suffering, and death lies bring. The job description of man was never meant to "be like God." It's hard enough being human.

Jumping to the ministry of Jesus, he confirms the source of lies in satanic spiritual reality. In a contentious engagement with the Pharisees in John 8 Jesus asserts the following.

> You belong to your father, the devil, and you want to carry out your father's desires. He was a murderer from the beginning, not holding to the truth, for there is no truth in him. When he lies, he speaks his native language, for he is a liar and the father of lies.

Lying is effectively a language indicating where someone comes from, to which country or nation they belong. As someone who speaks Japanese is likely from Japan, so someone who speaks lies is from hell. I'm not talking about someone who tells a little white lie, or someone who gets caught doing something and lies under pressure, but

CHAPTER 2

someone who lies as their "native language." As we've seen in the age of Trump, lies are the native language of the secular progressive left, a case that is not hard to make.

A full discussion of truth, a long, convoluted, and fascinating study in the history of ideas, is well beyond the scope of this book. But a basic understanding of how we got here is important if we're to understand why we live in such exciting times for the advancement of the Kingdom of God and the gospel.

For many Christians though, the times in which we live certainly don't seem to call for excitement. It appears to them, not unreasonably, that we're quickly heading to hell in a handbasket, ultimate disaster right around the corner. Many Christians will assure us we're certainly in "the end times." That topic, known as eschatology (the study of those end times), is something I will address later in the book, but the purpose of this chapter is to appreciate why truth, and its reality, has become the cultural touchstone of our present moment in history.

THE LAW OF NON-CONTRADICTION

We'll go back to ancient Greece and the Greek philosopher Aristotle who discovered the gift of logic in God's created reality. Foundational to logic, and thus reality, is the law of non-contradiction, or that opposite propositions cannot both be true at the same time and in the same sense; they cannot contradict one another. Put another way, A cannot be non-A. Something cannot "be" and "not be" simultaneously. Reality demands that nothing that is true can be true and self-contradictory or inconsistent with any other truth. All logic and rationality depend on this simple principle for without it meaningful discourse is impossible. To deny it is

THE DIVIDING LINE IN WESTERN CULTURE: THE TRUTH

to deny truth exists at all, like denying the sky is blue, or up is down and down is up, and the result is vertigo.

Francis Schaeffer in his 1968 book, *The God Who Is There*, said there was a chasm then between the generations brought on "almost entirely by a change in the concept of truth." What he said at the time was a drift in "the new way of looking at truth" had soon become a tsunami in 2020. He explained the concept of absolutes, that they exist and assume antithesis such as right and wrong, true and false.[3] Schaeffer wrote this before the rise of postmodernism in the 1970s and 80s, but he wouldn't be surprised that the obliteration of truth has made its way into every area of American and Western culture.

Richard Weaver in his 1948 book *Ideas Have Consequences* argues this obliteration went back to William of Ockham (1287–1347) and what Weaver called "the fateful doctrine of nominalism." Without getting into the details of the philos- ophy of nominalism itself, Weaver states:

> The issue ultimately involved is whether there is a source of truth higher than, and independent of, man; and the answer to the question is decisive for one's view of the nature and destiny of humankind…The denial of universals (nominalism) carries with it the denial of everything transcending experience…and means inevitably…the denial of truth. With the denial of objective truth there is no escape from the relativ- ism of "man the measure of all things." Thus began the "abomination of desolation" appearing today as a feeling of alienation from all fixed truth.

I'll repeat this was written in 1948, more than a decade before this "alienation from all fixed truth" exploded in what has come to be called "the Sixties." Even then, it would take more than half a century before Trump came down the escalator and the triumph of lies would reveal a dividing line in Western culture few in the seventeenth century could imagine when the Enlightenment got underway.

HOW THE ENLIGHTENMENT SET THE STAGE FOR THE TRIUMPH OF LIES

Epistemology is the study of how we know things, which became the focus of the Enlightenment, a period of Western history spanning the seventeenth and eighteenth centuries. Everyone who lived during that time, even the most skeptical among the intellectuals of the time, David Hume (1711-1776), believed in truth. The problem was what became known as rationalism. Most scholars would place the beginning of the Enlightenment and modern philosophy with René Descartes (1596-1650), although the antecedents went back to Ockham, and the empiricism of Francis Bacon (1561-1626).

History, however, is nothing if not ironic, and the worldview table was set for the destruction of truth by a pious Christian physicist every schoolchild knows, Sir Isaac Newton (1642-1727). Prior to Newton's physics, the people of Western Christian civilization saw nature as created and sustained by God. This biblical understanding of the material world led to the growth of science, but once Newton's physics became widely accepted, God became divorced from His own creation. Newtonian physics required nature to be seen as a closed and predictable system,[45] and the Western mind in due course saw nature as a vast mechanism that could run by itself. The implications of this shift will be especially apparent when we get to Darwin, but it started to have its effect in Newton's lifetime.

René Descartes, a pious Catholic Christian, was determined to challenge the growing skepticism of his day and decided to do that by doubting everything that could be doubted. He concluded the only thing he couldn't doubt was his thinking, and thus his existence. So, he made famous the phrase *Cogito Ergo Sum*, or I think therefore I am. The problem with what he thought was a universally self-evident truth, was in fact a distortion of truth, or to put it more bluntly, a lie. That "I think" is an indication of my existence, that "I am," but I do not exist *because* I think, but rather I exist because God created me—big difference. With Descartes, philosophy in Western thought made the consequential move from ontology, the study of being, to epistemology, how we know things. The prior focus, of necessity, started with God, the ground of being, *then* to us, while the latter started with us and knowing, and in due course ended there.

Thus, was born rationalism, or the notion that our thinking and reason is all that is necessary to know everything worth knowing. Revelation of God in Scripture was slowly but surely put to the side until the later eighteenth century when it became culturally acceptable to discredit it directly. Among intellectual elites, the Bible came to be seen as just another human book as liable to error as the humans who wrote it. Rationalism, however, proved to be a thin reed upon which to hang the entirety of human ability to know reality.

By the end of the eighteenth century the movement known as Romanticism started to push back against what was perceived as the cold analytical thinking of rationalism. It emphasized the individual and internal subjective experience over the objective external perception of things. Thinking gave way to feeling. The first philosopher who embodied this turn to the subjective was Jean-Jacques

Rousseau (1712-1778), however he died before it became a philosophical and cultural movement. Although a man of his age, he would have been right at home in the Sixties when hedonism became the norm in Western culture.

Unlike the "true for you, but not for me" relativists of the Sixties, those who embraced Romanticism would never claim truth didn't exist, only that it could not be discovered by reason alone. In that they were right and were as much a part of the "modern" world as the rationalists. The modern world was seen to contrast with the pre-modern world, known to some pejoratively as the Dark Ages, and to others as the Middle Ages. Before the modern world, man was supposedly caught up in superstition, things a truly modern person would never believe because they weren't discovered by reason alone.

Truth, however, was not so easily discovered by reason or feelings, as first believed. Hume realized reason alone could only lead ultimately to skepticism, or that knowledge wasn't possible. Giving up on knowledge wasn't something Western thinkers were willing to accept, so German philosopher Immanuel Kant (1724-1804) developed a convoluted and complicated philosophy to challenge skepticism and, he thought, save Christianity. The details of his philosophy are not important for our discussion, but we can conclude he was less than successful either in saving Christianity or saving truth for Western intellectuals.

Next in line for rationalism's slow demise was another German philosopher, Georg Wilhelm Friedrich Hegel (1770-1831), the father of historicism, or that all knowledge comes through the dialectic of history. First there is thesis, or some idea that comes through the historical process. Then there is an antithesis, or its opposite by the same process. When these two clash, there is synthesis, which becomes the next thesis, to be challenged by the next antithesis, and so on. It's a complicated and inscrutable philosophy, but the basic idea is rather simple. History is what reveals the nature of things, a world spirit ultimately finding its apotheosis in the state.

While few people have ever heard of Kant or Hegel, everyone knows our next two Western thinkers who built on the worldview of these philosophers among others, Charles Darwin (1809-1882) and Karl Marx (1818-1883). Deeply influenced by the reigning naturalism among the intellectuals of his time, Darwin posited evolution as a random material process that didn't require a Creator to account for the world and everything in it. Darwin's theory wasn't original, but his *Origin of Species* published in 1859 was exactly what Western intellectual elites hungered for so in short order they could declare in the infamous phrase of Friedrich Nietzsche (1844-1900), "God is dead, and we killed him." The impact of Darwin on the growing secularism of Western civilization and culture cannot be overestimated, but it was Marx who took the worldview bequeathed to him and whose influence eventually turned it into a massive killing machine in the twentieth century. We will deal with Marx in some detail in the next chapter, but we'll use the analogy of a vacuum to look at what these two men accomplished.

The phrase "nature abhors a vacuum" goes back to Aristotle, so when God was no longer needed to explain the world, something had to explain it, to fill the vacuum. Darwin did that. In his book *The Blind Watchmaker*, outspoken atheist Richard Dawkins declared that "Darwin made it possible to be an intellectually fulfilled atheist," not to mention the full-blown secularism we live in today. The vacuum that Marx filled was a theodicy, or more typically stated as the problem of evil. Marx didn't invent the term communism, but it was his writing that did more to popularize it than anyone else. The rise of industrialism in the nineteenth century brought much misery with it, and Marx's ideas for many were a plausible explanation of suffering in a God-less world. Truth, however, survived both Darwin and Marx, but it met its match in the man we come to next.

FRIEDRICH NIETZSCHE AND THE RISE OF POSTMODERNISM

As the term postmodernism indicates, it came after modernism. A defining feature of the latter is that it believed in truth and that truth was worth seeking and knowable by reason alone, while the postmodernists rejected this premise of modernist epistemology. Both are fundamentally secular and embrace naturalism, rejecting the Creator God, and thus have no metaphysical justification for the existence of truth.

This logical inconsistency didn't keep modernists from believing in truth, but it was Nietzsche's hostility to modernism that made him possibly the first postmodernist, even though he believed in truth every bit as much as they did. Christian Philosopher Douglas Groothuis in his book *Truth Decay*, says:

> It is difficult to identify one philosopher who marks the transition from modernism to postmodernism, but Friedrich Nietzsche is probably the top candidate... [he] saw "the death of God" as having profound consequences for every area of thought and culture. He had little patience with Enlightenment philosophers who removed God from their belief systems yet retained belief in Christian moral principles

and an orderly, rational universe. The end of theism brought with it the end of objective value, meaning and significance; altruism has no basis in a universal moral law; the will to power was the essential fact in the struggle to thrive . . .[6]

This is an excellent synopsis of Nietzsche, and one of the most "profound consequences" is the destruction of truth. Without the metaphysical grounding of God, truth floats off into the air like easily popped bubbles from a child's toy. The postmodernists took the atheism Nietzsche assumed to its logical conclusion; for them all so-called truth is mere bubbles, or what they called metanarratives. A metanarrative is a story a culture tells itself about its beliefs and practices, but it is only a story, never the truth about the nature of things. Such truth, to them, doesn't exist.

The irony of Nietzsche is that he believed in truth passionately but opened the door to its decay in Western culture. Walter Kaufmann wrote of the realization Nietzsche came to about God's demise:

> Nietzsche prophetically envisages himself as a madman; to have lost God means madness; and when mankind will discover that it has lost God, universal madness will break out. This apocalyptic sense of dreadful things to come hangs over Nietzsche's thinking like a thundercloud. We have destroyed our own faith in God. There remains only the void. We are falling. Our dignity is gone. Our values are lost. Who is to say what is up and what is down.[7]

Mind you, Nietzsche was convinced we live in a God-less universe because he uncritically accepted all the materialist assumptions of the Enlightenment. It was rationalism he found distasteful, and the failure of modernists to accept the implications of what they believed. Because God was dead, and the "slave morality," as he called it, of Christianity was no longer valid, a new moral system needed to be developed, and he was just the man to do it! Thus, his ideas of the "will to power" and the *Übermensch*, or overman, were critical to developing an alternative moral system.

The details of such a system are not relevant to our discussion, but Nietzsche was convinced that man properly understood could create something far superior to Christianity. In effect, the metanarrative of Christianity that had served Western civilization must be replaced. In due course, however, the death of God inevitably led to the death of truth in Western culture, and true for you, but not for me relativism eventually won the day. This is what Schaeffer was referring to when he lamented the death of absolutes, of antithesis, and the law of non-contradiction.

Whether relativism or postmodernism came first is a chicken-and-egg debate, but both are inevitable with the death of God. In the 1970s, French intellectuals like Jacques Derrida, Michel Foucault, and Jean-François Lyotard made postmodernism a thing, and "the narrative" became a dominant theme of the left. Truth became the enemy of "the narrative" of the ruling elites, and "the narrative" was the enemy of truth. I was introduced to these ideas when I was in college in the late '70s, and thought it was ridiculous. I had no idea one day they would permeate Western culture like an invisible monster. Fortunately, many people are now realizing that the monster doesn't even exist.

THE METAPHYSICAL & SPIRITUAL
IMPLICATIONS OF TRUTH

This brings me to truth as dividing line. As I said above, because truth is a person and not merely the nature of things, those things point to The Truth, the person of God in Christ. The kingdom of God is the kingdom of Truth, and those who embrace truth are in some way connected to that kingdom, and in our time that includes many people who do not embrace Christianity. The liberals whom I talked about being red-pilled in the first chapter are all committed to truth over narrative, and in a profound way are on our side in this war for Christian Western civilization.

In contrast to these truth-committed liberals, the post-modern left has embraced Nietzsche's will to power, not just in their tyrannical use of government and law, but in words as well. Lying to protect and project their political ideology has become more important than a truth they really don't believe in anyway. What is true and what is a lie doesn't matter to them; "the narrative" is all.

The awakened, red-pilled liberals have realized what I saw on a bumper sticker at church some years ago: "Truth is treason in an empire of lies." Many liberals have been shocked to learn that "In a time of universal deceit, telling the truth is a revolutionary act" (a quote attributed to George Orwell, but likely not his). Selwyn Duke put it well, "The further a society drifts from Truth, the more it will hate those who speak it."[8] These red-pilled liberals have taken the challenge of Aleksandr Solzhenitsyn to his fellow Russians enslaved by communism to heart: "Live Not by Lies."[9]

I often use the metaphor of the Berlin Wall for secular leftist progressivism, and the globalist technocratic state it

31

champions. This wall will also come tumbling down because it is all built on lies, and an empire built on lies cannot stand. It is destined for the same ash-heap as Ronald Reagan declared of the Soviet Union ten years before its demise:

> What I am describing now is a plan and a hope for the long term—the march of freedom and democracy which will leave Marxism-Leninism on the ash-heap of history, as it has left other tyrannies which stifle the freedom and muzzle the self-expression of the people.[10]

Most of us thought this was wishful thinking. "It would be nice, Ronnie, but not in our lifetimes." Then five years later, on June 12, 1987, Reagan doubled down on his conviction of the inherent frailty of the Soviet communist state by challenging the Soviet General Secretary, "Mr. Gorbachev, tear down this wall!" Now, we thought, Ronnie's really lost it. Yet, less than two years later, the Wall came down.

The remorseless tide of reality mocked the pretensions of communism even as it now mocks the pretensions of secular progressive religion; when the tide goes out, it's clear who is wearing bathing suits and who isn't. Those with the bathing suits on, those committed to the truth no matter the cost, are what we call co-belligerents in the existential culture war for Christian Western civilization in which we are now engaged. They are on our side, the side of truth, the side of the kingdom of God. This not only has metaphysical implications in a philosophical sense, but also in a spiritual sense.

Before we can go there, to where we are and where we are going, we need to have a serious discussion about God's providence.

CHAPTER 3

A THEOLOGY OF HISTORY AND THE PROVIDENCE OF GOD

If my claim of Trump being the trigger for a Great Awakening is to carry any water, I must establish God as the one who gave us Trump in this place, this time, and in this way. Some Christians might recoil at such an assertion, but it is the only conclusion for Christians who believe in a sovereign, almighty God. Biblically there is no other option.

Theoretically, all Christians believe in God's providence, the idea that history is *His* story. He calls the shots. He determines what does and does not happen. How He does so is not our concern because, well, He is God and we are not. I say theoretically because of the powerful influence of the all-pervasive secularism of our age. We're so used to secularism we have no idea how much it infects our view of everything and how easily we see things as a secularist might instead of as a Christian should. Our view of history is one of the casualties.

To my dismay several years ago I discovered how susceptible I am to this malady, in this case related to the "natural" world. I came across a claim by C.S. Lewis I'd never considered because, like everyone else, I am programmed to see the world as if naturalism were true, as if some things were just "natural" and God isn't required to make them work.

Mind you, I know God is required for everything, but secularism's influence is subtle and deceptive. Lewis stated that Mary's conception by the Holy Spirit was no more miraculous than any woman's conceiving.[1] I had never considered this. Is not a new being's creation utterly miraculous? Are we really supposed to believe the process of creating a new life is solely "natural"? No divine assistance required? How about a seed in the ground? Is it only dirt, air, water, and sun that causes it to grow? No. The answer is God! Those things are necessary, as are all secondary causes, but the primary cause of all things is God, including history.

A BIBLICAL VIEW OF HISTORY

Like most Christians influenced by secularism, I've tended to see history and events like hurricanes just happening and who knows which way either one will go. In September 2022, when Hurricane Ian was tracking toward where we live in the Tampa area, I had to remind myself it is God alone who determines where it goes, not mere "natural" forces. Regarding history, we often must remind ourselves that God directs all events, past, present, and future.

A proper Christian providential theology of history is captured by Daniel when God revealed to him Nebuchadnezzar's Dream. Grateful he and his buddies would not be killed, he proclaims the greatness of our God, the author and director not only of our faith (Heb. 12:2), but of all history:

> Then Daniel praised the God of heaven [20] and said:
> "Praise be to the name of God for ever and ever;
>   wisdom and power are his.
> [21] He changes times and seasons;
>   he deposes kings and raises up others.

> He gives wisdom to the wise
>   and knowledge to the discerning.

In Daniel 4, after Nebuchadnezzar's sanity was restored, this pagan king of Babylon also couldn't help coming to the same conclusion as Daniel the Hebrew prophet:

> Then I praised the Most High; I honored and glorified him who lives forever
> His dominion is an eternal dominion;
>   his kingdom endures from generation to generation.
> [35] All the peoples of the earth
>   are regarded as nothing.
> He does as he pleases
>   with the powers of heaven
>   and the peoples of the earth.
> No one can hold back his hand
>   or say to him: "What have you done?"

For Christians I don't need to belabor the point other than to say, *what in the world are we worried about!* Jesus commanded us not to worry about anything. Does it mean things won't get scary, or fear is never warranted? They sometimes will, and yes, it is scary, but maybe the answer to those questions isn't so simple.

I chuckle when I read about Jesus calming the storm and asking his disciples, "Why are you afraid?" That seems like a ridiculous question unless Jesus *was* God in human flesh, then it's a perfectly reasonable question. Or when Peter walks on water on a storm-tossed lake, sees the wind, and fear kicks in. He starts sinking, and terrified he screams for Jesus to save him. Jesus does, then calmly says, "You of little faith, why did you doubt?" *Oh, I don't know, Jesus, maybe because human beings can't walk on water!!* If Jesus was God in human flesh, however, doubt might not be warranted, and walking on water was in fact possible. I would suggest we look at current events and contemplate the future in obedience to Jesus, without fear.

The Apostles Creed declares our belief in God, the Father almighty, Creator of heaven and earth, and then we affirm the second person of the Trinity:

> I believe in Jesus Christ, his only Son, our Lord,
> who was conceived by the Holy Spirit
> and born of the virgin Mary.
> He suffered under Pontius Pilate,
> was crucified, died, and was buried;
> he descended to hell.
> The third day he rose again from the dead.
> He ascended to heaven
> and is seated at the right hand of God the Father almighty.
> From there he will come to judge the living and the dead.

We Evangelicals do not pay enough attention to Christ's ascension. I realized this a few years ago when listening to a podcast, and the speaker mentioned that it is almost an afterthought for most of us. The resurrection is what really counts, of course. The church was built and grew on that claim, but Jesus went somewhere after He rose from the dead, ascending to heaven and the right hand of the Father. In the ancient world the one who sat at the right hand of the king shared his kingly authority and power. In this case, Jesus has the ultimate position of power and authority in the universe.

The crowning New Testament rationale for the confidence of Daniel and Nebuchadnezzar in God's providence in history is found in Ephesians 1. We cannot overemphasize the theological and providential implications of Christ's ascension, and Paul tells us why. Speaking of the surpassing greatness of the power for those who trust the Lord Jesus, he says:

> That power is the same as the mighty strength [20] he exerted when he raised Christ from the dead and seated him at his right hand in the heavenly realms, [21] far above all rule and authority, power and dominion, and every name that is invoked, not only in the present age but also in the one to come. [22] And God placed all things under his feet and appointed him to be head over everything for the church, [23] which is his body, the fullness of him who fills everything in every way.

This is not only the rule and authority of material creation, but over beings spiritual *and* mortal that exercise rule and authority and power and dominion—over *all* of them. Many Christians quote Paul's declaration in Ephesians 6:12: "For our struggle is not against flesh and blood, but against the rulers, against the authorities, against the powers of this dark world and against the spiritual forces of evil in the heavenly realms." But it is critical to quote this in the context of the passage in Ephesians 1. Nothing happens that Christ doesn't permit or cause to happen; His rule is sovereign and absolute.

Like most Christians, however, I tended to see this passage eschatologically because as Christians we know how the story ends. It's more difficult to grasp that Jesus has all this power *now* and is using it in *this* world, in space and time, for the advancement of His kingdom and ultimately for His church. This has implications beyond the church, though, which is why Paul tells us Jesus' kingly rule is not just for the age to come, but for the present age as well.

LINEAR VERSUS TELEOLOGICAL VIEW OF HISTORY

Once we accept God's providential control over history, we need to have some idea how it works out in actual history, as in what the implications are for history.

Prior to "In the beginning God created the heavens and the earth" (Gen. 1), all ancient peoples viewed time cyclically, a perpetual wheel endlessly turning going nowhere. Thomas Cahill says one of the most profound changes Jews brought to the ancient world was the conception of time and history. This change started when God called Abram to go from Ur of the Chaldeans to the land of Canaan, by *faith* he left everything he knew, and the world was forever changed:

> Faith supplants the generalized predictability of the ancient world with the possibility of both real success and real failure, real happiness and real tragedy—that is, a real journey whose outcome is not yet...Cyclical religion goes nowhere because within its comprehension, there is no future as we have come to understand it, only the next revolution of the wheel. Since time is no longer cyclical but one-way and irreversible, personal history is now possible and an individual life can have value.[2]

Many Christians tend to think the contrast to the cyclical view of history is linear, a line going straight in one direction from A to B. That, however, is not the biblical understanding of history. If we've learned anything from thousands of years of recorded history, it's anything but straight. It zigs and zags all over the place, backward, forward, and sideways. Biblically, the contrast to cyclical isn't linear but teleological. This word comes from the Greek *telos* meaning purpose or end. In this understanding of history, every event is leading somewhere regardless of what it may look like on the surface. Vern Poythress explains:

> The Bible does give us a framework for the whole of history. This framework is there even when we do not explicitly acknowledge it. God has his purposes. The purposes are there eternally, from before the foundation of the world, and are worked out in the unfolding of particular events. The Bible also tells us about the goal of history. Every event has significance not only because of God's plan, which lies at the origin, but because of God's purpose for the end. Every event contributes to the process leading to an end, the consummation in Christ, the new heavens and the new earth.[3]

This means there are no throwaway events in history, things that just happen. I agree with Poythress that every event has teleological significance whether we think we can see it or not. Too often we presume that we can. There are many times looking back in history, or at current events, or even in our own lives, when this is difficult to swallow. The most common question in all of history attests to this, "Why, God?" It just doesn't make any sense...to us.

Whenever I wonder this myself, I look back through Scripture and see how often biblical characters felt the same way. The examples are numerous, but one of the most powerful is the time between the crucifixion and the resurrection. Jesus' disciples were convinced He was the 400-years-long awaited Messiah of Israel. The expectations for this Davidic conqueror over Israel's enemies didn't include Him being ignominiously crucified on a Roman cross, to say the least. What made it even worse was Jesus being hung on a tree. According to Deuteronomy 21:23, He was under God's curse. For the disciples, this would have been deeply disturbing. I can imagine them wondering in their pain, how Jesus could have lied to them.

Keep in mind it wasn't the resurrection itself that allowed His death on a cross to eventually make sense. To first century Jews, a resurrection of one man in the middle of history was inconceivable, but it was also incomprehensible. It made no more sense than the crucifixion. Prior to giving the eleven disciples the Great Commission, we get a sense of just how incomprehensible (Matt. 28):

> When they saw him, they worshiped him; but some doubted.

The dead guy who was brutally tortured and killed is now alive and talking to them, but they still can't wrap their Jewish minds around it.

It was only after He was resurrected and explained to His disciples (Luke 24) the ultimate biblical hermeneutical principal—that the entire Old Testament was about Him—that it started to become plausible. This is the same hermeneutical principle for all history: we interpret it all according to God's revealed word. Because of this, we can no longer look at the past, present, and future, and all events contained therein, in any other way. They are all ultimately

about Jesus in some way, unless we have some other inter-
pretive non-biblical framework for history.

THE SECULAR VIEW OF HISTORY

Those who don't have a biblical and thus providential view
of history will by default have a secular one. Even though
there are variations on the secular view, a strictly God-
less interpretation of history means there is no overarching
narrative, no *telos* to history. Things happen randomly. If
there is no God ordaining and guiding history providentially,
we're forced to conclude it is but chance and agree with
Macbeth at the death of his wife:

> Tomorrow, and tomorrow, and tomorrow
> Creeps in this petty pace from day to day
> To the last syllable of recorded time.
> And all our yesterdays have lighted fools
> The way to dusty death. Out, out, brief candle.
> Life's but a walking shadow, a poor player
> That struts and frets his hour upon the stage,
> And then is heard no more. It is a tale
> Told by an idiot, full of sound and fury,
> Signifying nothing.

Typical of Shakespeare, it could not be said any better.
However, given we cannot escape living in God's created
universe no matter how hard sinful humanity insists otherwise, chance has never proved a satisfying explanation, for
anything. We also live with thousands of years of the influence of Judaism and Christianity, so the teleological view

of history can't be completely escaped. Which brings us to Hegel.

We briefly looked at German philosopher Georg Wilhelm Friedrich Hegel as the father of historicism in the last chapter. He espoused a teleological view of history *without* God—well, without a god any of us might recognize. Having been raised a Christian, Hegel believed in God, but having accepted Enlightenment rationalism without question, a personal God who ordains history according to His will was out of the question. Instead, his God was history itself as the unfolding of a World-Spirit. It's impossible to understand what was going on in the mind of a genius like Hegel, but Frederick Copleston gives it a try:

> World-history is the process whereby Spirit comes to actual consciousness of itself as freedom. Hence 'world-history is progress in the consciousness of freedom'. This consciousness is attained, of course, only in and through the mind of man. And the divine Sprit, as manifested in history through the consciousness of man, is the World-Spirit. History, therefore, is the process whereby the World-Spirit comes to explicit consciousness of itself as free.[4]

If that doesn't make sense to you, join the club. Somehow it made sense to Hegel, and apparently to a lot of other philosophers and intellectuals, including one Karl Marx. I've always been fascinated by the history of ideas, and how ideas inscrutable to normal people, like most of what Hegel wrote, make their way into the culture and influence history. On that count, Hegel is one of the most influential thinkers of the modern world.

I mentioned the word historicism, which is a bastard-ization of the Christian idea of God's providence. Hegel, who considered himself a Christian, thought he was saving Christianity in the age of Enlightenment. Needless to say, he didn't do a good job. Copleston tells us what Hegel thought he was doing:

> My point is that Hegel's metaphysics drives him to the conclusions to which the Christian theologian is not committed. True, Hegel thought that he was giving the philosophical essence, as it were, of the Christian doctrine of providence. But in point of fact this 'demythologization' was a transformation.[5]

Transformation indeed!

I did a search for some simple definitions of historicism to give us an idea of what Hegel's ideas might mean in a more concrete way for our discussion of secular "provi-dence." Here are a few that I found:

- A theory that events are determined or influenced by conditions and inherent processes beyond the control of humans.
- The belief that natural laws govern historical events which in turn determine social and cultural phenomena.
- A theory that history is determined by immutable laws and not by human agency.

These ideas only have a tangential connection to the Christian understanding of providence, but in a completely distorted way. In the Christian view, human beings have real agency; they can change things even though God ordains and is in control of all things. We can cite many passages in Scripture, but one comes to mind in Acts 2:

> [22] "Fellow Israelites, listen to this: Jesus of Nazareth was a man accredited by God to you by miracles, wonders and signs, which God did among you through him, as you yourselves know. [23] This man was handed over to you by God's deliberate plan and foreknowledge; and you, with the help of wicked men, put him to death by nailing him to the cross.

As you consider the implications of historicism, however it is defined, it bears little resemblance to God's providence in ordaining the crucifixion of the Son of God. It was God's "deliberate" plan, but it was men who of their own volition committed the act, thus they are accountable for those acts.

The most common way historicism is embraced is historical determinism, which downplays human agency and accountability. President Obama often used the phrase, "the wrong side of history" because he wanted to make a connection with Martin Luther King's precept that "the arc of the moral universe is long, but it bends toward justice." This quote was so important to Obama he had it literally woven into a rug in the Oval Office. Of course, this depends on who or whatever is doing the bending. King clearly believed that was God; Obama, I'm not so sure, given his commitment to radical leftist politics.

Aside from political considerations, most people tend to think "progress" is baked into the historical cake. A driving assumption is that things just naturally get better because as secularism teaches, we went from ancient superstition and "the dark ages" to Enlightenment and science. The secular Western idea of "progress" is something we'll explore in more detail, but Western secularists think progress is a human birthright. What could go wrong? The 20th century!

THE SECULAR ESCHATOLOGY OF DOOM

Until the early twentieth century, everything was Mr. Rogers' Neighborhood. Sing it with me, "It's a beautiful day in the neighborhood..." Uh, maybe not. Living in the twenty-first century it's difficult to imagine how hard life was for the vast majority of populations in Western nations during the nineteenth century. Yet an infectious optimism gripped the imaginations of all but the most downtrodden. Industrialization brought a new kind of misery to cities exploding in growth, but the blessings of technology and knowledge were undeniable. To cite only one of those blessings, clean water was brought to the masses and saved untold lives from disease because of indoor plumbing and public sanitation.

A good example of the understandable hubris of the time was the 1893 Chicago World's Fair. Held around the world annually, fairs showcased some the world's most revolutionary inventions and concepts known at the time, and the period between 1880 and World War I was the golden age of fairs. At the Chicago fair, known as the World's Columbian Exposition celebrating Columbus' arrival in the New World in 1492, the world-changing technology of electric light made its debut. It really seemed humanity could accomplish anything and conquer the limits imposed by nature. Without God, however, as Nietzsche prophesied, disaster loomed.

Although a staunch atheist, Nietzsche realized Christianity had created the moral framework that made *Christian* Western civilization possible, and without something in its place, bad things were bound to happen. Branches can't be cut from the tree and live. According to Walter Kauffmann, Nietzsche's writings abound in prophecies of doom.

> "If the doctrines . . . of the lack of any cardinal distinction between man and animal . . . are hurled into the people for another generation," if mankind realizes the unique worth of the human being has evaporated, and that no up and down remains, and if the tremendous event that we have killed God reaches the ears of man—then night will close in, "an age of barbarism begins," and "there will be wars such as have never happened on earth."[6]

Next to this paragraph in the book I wrote, "The 20th Century!!!" And remember, this comes from a convinced atheist, but one who realized the West wasn't just cutting off branches but cutting down the entire tree! It's safe to say, no other thinker at the time would have said anything like this, and his prescient prophecies proved disastrously true.

I place the beginning of the end of modernism and its inevitable secularism with the sinking of RMS Titanic in April 1912. While the builders and White Star Line, the technological marvel's operator, never actually declared it unsinkable, that was the impression in popular imagination. The sinking was a huge cultural blow to the dominant hubris of the time. A little more than two years later a war of unimaginable horror and carnage swept up the most educated and civilized nations in the world. This "war to end all wars" had many horrific unintended consequences, as all wars do, and two decades later led to an even more deadly and horrendous war. One of those consequences was the Russian Revolution, leading to Soviet communism and tens of millions more dead. The communists seemed to want to outdo each other in the mass murder sweepstakes, and Mao, Pol Pot, Castro, and others gave the world by most estimates north of 100 million corpses. An "age of barbarism" only begins to describe it.

Ironically, despite all the carnage and destruction, Western cultural and political leaders were more confident than ever "progress" would continue. Technocratic man and "scientific management" would solve all problems sooner or later. The post–World War II period was an especially heady time. People in the 1950s and early 1960s pre–Vietnam believed anything was possible. Kennedy's administration was staffed with the "best and the brightest," young guns who never doubted their ability to do great things with their power. Kennedy's promise of landing a man on the moon in 1961 was indicative of the can-do spirit. Under the surface, however, cracks were beginning to appear.

Technology, like anything sinful human beings create, can be used for good or evil. As Blaise Pascal put it so memorably:

> Man's greatness and wretchedness are so evident that the true religion must necessarily teach us that there is in man some great principle of greatness and some great principle of wretchedness.[7]

The cracks leading to the eschatological doom I speak of started with the 1962 book by Rachal Carson called *Silent Spring*, which set the stage for the environmental movement.

She exposed the hazards of the pesticide DDT, and questioned humanity's faith in unlimited technological progress. In due course, environmental doom and gloom became a staple of the left's worldview. Global warming transmogrified into "climate change," and is only the latest catastrophe awaiting mankind if radical revolutionary changes are not enacted. These changes just happen to conveniently require globalist, leftist, tyrannical, anti-free enterprise solutions, always top down, never bottom up.

THE INFLUENCE OF CHRISTIAN ESCHATOLOGY

It's important to remember the concept of eschatology, of history going somewhere with an inherent telos, is a solely Jewish/Christian concept. Providence, however bastardized it becomes, is an inescapable influence of Christianity. Every worldview influenced by Christianity has an eschatology, a vision of the end of things, including secularism, and given the obvious dysfunction of the world, they inevitably tend towards the negative.

Which brings us to the Book of Revelation. Any providential discussion of history, including now and the history to come, can't escape the most influential biblical book in Western history, eschatology or not. It's instructive to consider the Greek word John uses for revelation as he begins his letter to "the seven churches in the province of Asia." His first words are, "The revelation of Jesus Christ..." The word is *apokálypsis* and simply means unveiling, uncovering, revealing, revelation, and has no inherent positive or negative connotation. The word in English as it has come down to us, apocalypse, has only negative meaning when we see, hear, or use it ourselves. That is the influence of a certain interpretation of Revelation, as we'll explore in detail in a later chapter, but left or right, secular or religious, what often unites them all is the conviction the worst is yet to come.

Before we explore why I disagree with that and how we got where we are in the twenty-first century, it is hard to deny the worst is in fact happening. We must remember, however, that despite much ugliness and suffering in American history, until recently most Americans and their leaders viewed God's providence hopefully. Even today, politicians can't be Debbie Downers and expect to win. To that we'll turn next.

CHAPTER 4

AMERICA'S PROVIDENTIAL VIEW OF HISTORY

The biblical providential view of history has been an important part of the American experience. America's peculiarity, what some have called American exceptionalism, appears to have divine footprints all over it, and most Americans believed that until the mid-twentieth century. In hindsight, it's easy to see how this has been used for good and ill. For example, both North and South were convinced that God and His providence was on their side.

The phrase "manifest destiny" is a fascinating example of both, written almost as a throwaway line by John L. O'Sullivan, the editor of a Democrat Party magazine. In a long piece penned for the magazine in 1845 supporting the Mexican American war, O'Sullivan argued for the need to annex Texas and the inevitability of American expansion across the continent. He wrote about France and England interfering in American affairs:

> "[F]or the avowed object of thwarting our policy and hampering our power, limiting our greatness, and checking the fulfillment of our manifest destiny to overspread the continent allotted by Providence for the free development of our yearly multiplying millions."

Later that year, writing a much shorter piece in the *New York Morning News,* O'Sullivan again asserted:

> "[T]he right of our manifest destiny to overspread and to possess the whole of the continent which Providence has given us for the development of the great experiment of liberty and federated self-government entrusted to us."

Providence meant God, and something manifest is clearly apparent. Notice the word "entrusted." God's providence wasn't an excuse to abuse our destiny as Americans, but to responsibly fulfill it.

By that point in the nineteenth century, it was clear to any observer the destiny of America was to spread over the entire continent. By 1845, the phrase manifest destiny was axiomatic, if not widely used. It quickly became controversial, however, but it may surprise us that it was Democrats who pushed it. Today, anyone suggesting American exceptionalism, such as manifest destiny implies, is vehemently denounced as a xenophobe by modern Democrats. Regardless of the details of the nineteenth century controversies, God and His providence were part of the discussion. Until the poisonous flower of secularism fully bloomed in the 1960s, God was a welcome guest in American public life. After that, not so much.

THE FOUNDING GENERATION AND AMERICA'S PROVIDENTIAL VIEW OF HISTORY

None of the Founding Generation would be surprised where the experiment in American republican government currently finds itself, but neither would it cause them to reject a providential view of history rooted in the Bible. While not all of America's Founders were Christians, all of them had a biblical worldview to one degree or another. None of the Founders, as is often claimed, were truly Deists, believing in a clock-making God who sets creation going and doesn't intervene in its history. And none of them were secularists. A view of reality devoid of divine providence would have been as foreign to them as divine providence is to modern secularists. Henry F. May in his book, *The Enlightenment in America*, identifies four different Enlightenment traditions, and America's was of the moderate sort.[1] Speaking of the roots of American culture at the time, May writes:

> One of these consists of the doctrines of Protestantism and particularly Calvinistic Protestantism, drawn from sixteenth- and seventeenth-century Europe but developed and institutionalized with great vigor in America particularly in New England. The other cluster of ideas is drawn from the Enlightenment of seventeenth and eighteenth-century Europe. The relation between these two major idea systems is basic to the understanding of eighteenth-century America, and indeed, I would say, the understanding of America in any period.

That is still true today in our secular age in ways that might surprise us but is beyond the scope of this book.

Unlike the skeptical and revolutionary Enlightenment traditions, America's Founding generation embraced Christianity as a positive good for society without which it couldn't survive. The Christian God of the Bible was an integral part of the founding of the republic, and they believed His providence was instrumental in allowing it to happen.

The final words of the Declaration of Independence make this clear:

> And for the support of this Declaration, with a firm reliance on the protection of divine Providence, we mutually pledge to each other our lives, our fortunes and our sacred honor.

This theology of the Declaration of America's independence from Britain was written by one of the least orthodox Christians of the bunch, Thomas Jefferson, and supposedly one of the most Deist. Yet Jefferson's God did not appear to be Deist at all but was intimately involved with his creation. He starts the document with a reference to the Laws of Nature and of Nature's God, phraseology that was not uncommon in the eighteenth century. He next declared those familiar words, that "all men are created equal, that they are endowed by their Creator with certain unalienable Rights, that among these are Life, Liberty and the pursuit of Happiness." The God of the Bible was the God of America's Founding.

Another of the supposedly confirmed founding Deists, Benjamin Franklin, likewise doesn't appear to believe in a clockmaker God. He makes that clear in his speech to the Constitutional Convention on June 28, 1787:

> I've lived, Sir, a long time, and the longer I live, the more convincing Proofs I see of this Truth—That God governs in the Affairs of Men. And if a sparrow cannot fall to the ground without his Notice, is it probable that an Empire can rise without his Aid? We have been assured, Sir, in the Sacred Writings, that except the Lord build the House they labor in vain who build it. I firmly believe this,—and I also believe that without

his concurring Aid, we shall succeed in this political Building no better than the Builders of Babel: We shall be divided by our little partial local interests; our Projects will be confounded, and we ourselves shall become a Reproach and Bye word down to future Ages.

These could be the words of any orthodox Calvinist of the time.

Or take America's first president, George Washington, also not the most orthodox of Christians. On November 25, 1789, he stated the following in his Thanksgiving Proclamation:

Whereas it is the duty of all Nations to acknowledge the providence of Almighty God, to obey his will, to be grateful for his benefits, and humbly to implore his protection and favor – and whereas both Houses of Congress have by their joint Committee requested me to recommend to the People of the United States a day of public thanksgiving and prayer to be observed by acknowledging with grateful hearts the many signal favors of Almighty God especially by affording them an opportunity peaceably to establish a form of government for their safety and happiness.

We could say the same about John Adams, second president of the United States, and no raging Evangelical. He was convinced that without religion, i.e., Christianity, America could not be a successful self-governing republic. One of his more famous quotations makes this clear:

Our Constitution was made only for a moral and religious people. It is wholly inadequate to the government of any other.

This was affirmed by Congress six months before the Constitution was passed in the Northwest Ordinance of 1787. In Article 3 it states:

> Religion, morality, and knowledge, being necessary to good government and the happiness of mankind, schools and the means of education shall forever be encouraged.

The Founders believed it was the Christian religion and Christian morality of a providentially ordaining God that made the American experiment possible.

It wasn't just America's political leaders who believed Christianity was integral to America's founding, but its religious leaders as well. In fact, many argue the first Great Awakening of the 1730s and 1740s associated with men like Edwards, Wesley, and Whitefield created the necessary conditions for the Revolution. Unlike today when many Evangelical ministers are hesitant to preach on politics, minsters of the Founding era had no such qualms. I have a book on my shelf called, *Political Sermons of the American Founding Era: 1730-1805*, and it clocks in at nearly 1,600 pages! Unlike the over-spiritualized Christianity of much modern Evangelicalism, Christians had no problem applying their faith in the public arena. Editor Ellis Sandoz in the foreword gives a sense of the comprehensive nature of the Christian worldview of the ministers of that generation:

> [A] steady attention to the pulpit unveils a distinctive rhetoric of political discourse: Preachers interpreted pragmatic events in terms of a political theology imbued with philosophical and revelatory learning. Their sermons also demonstrate the existence

and effectiveness of a popular political culture that constantly assimilated the currently urgent political and constitutional issues to the profound insights of the Western spiritual and philosophical traditions. The culture's political theorizing within the compass of ultimate historical and metaphysical concerns gave clear contours to secular events in the minds of Americans in this vital era.[2]

In other words, unlike in our day, politics was seen as a profoundly spiritual undertaking that required the deepest spiritual and philosophical insight. They wouldn't think of dismissing something as "just politics."

In addition, both religious and political leaders saw Christianity as necessary for religious and political liberty as well. James Madison, an Evangelical Christian who studied at the College of New Jersey under John Witherspoon, a Presbyterian minister and signer of the Declaration of Independence, said in 1785:

> Before any man can be considered as a member of Civil Society, he must be considered as a subject of the Governour of the Universe.

And this was in an address defending religious liberty. The Founders believed that religious liberty and Christianity were inseparable. Madison argued for the freedom of conscience that started with Martin Luther's famous declaration at the Diet (Assembly) of Worms in 1521. Commanded to repudiate his writings, he stood against an array of powerful clergy and statesmen asserting he could not go against his conscience. The official transcript quotes him as saying:

Unless I am convicted by Scripture and plain reason (I do not accept the authority of popes and councils because they have contradicted each other), my conscience is captive to the Word of God. I cannot and will not recant anything, for to go against conscience is neither right nor safe. So help me God. Amen.

In Luther's collected works his closing words come down to us most famously as, "Here I stand, I can do no other, so help me God. Amen." This affirmation of conscience was the first such declaration in Western history, and nothing thereafter would be the same. A little over a hundred years later, a primary motivation of Oliver Cromwell in the English Civil War against King Charles I was freedom of conscience and religious toleration.[3] They fought for "the rights of Englishmen" from which the Founders drew inspiration but took to another level we can better recognize.

The commitment of the Founders to religious liberty and freedom of conscience is well-trod ground, but it is imperative to continually emphasize it because the dominant religion of our age, secularism, pits Christianity against liberty, as if Christianity taken seriously leads to perpetual wars of religion. Secularists are fine with Christianity as long as it remains a purely private matter, having no claim on the public square. As soon as Christians assert claims to public morality and governance, the secularists cry theocracy! In fact, the current tyrannical theocracy in America is secularism.

LINCOLN, THE CIVIL WAR, AND GOD'S PROVIDENCE

We could multiply quotes about Christianity, God, and religion in the Founding era, but it isn't necessary. God was an important consideration for all presidents and political and cultural leaders in the nineteenth century as well, given Christianity was the dominant worldview.

I want to next move to the Civil War era, and how God was a significant player in the drama. I'm not sure there was anything more hellish in Western history than then half a million citizens of a country dying at the hands of their fellow citizens in a civil war. Yet God was continually invoked to try to explain the unexplainable. Nobody did that better than Lincoln.

In his powerful first inaugural address, he lays out the case with poetical power:

> Why should there not be a patient confidence in the ultimate justice of the people? Is there any better or equal hope in the world? In our present differences is either party without faith of being in the right? If the Almighty Ruler of Nations, with his eternal truth and justice, be on your side of the North, or on yours of the South, that truth and that justice will surely prevail by the judgment of this great tribunal of the American people... Intelligence, patriotism, Christianity, and a firm reliance on Him who has never yet forsaken this favored land, are still competent to adjust in the best way all our present difficulty.

Even America's Founders knew slavery would one day have to be paid for. George Mason of Virginia warned of the judgment of God if slavery was allowed to continue:

> Every master is born a petty tyrant. They bring the judgment of Heaven upon a country. As nations cannot be rewarded or punished in the next world, they

must be in this. By an inevitable chain of causes and effects, Providence punishes national sins by national calamities.

Jefferson agreed. In Notes on The State of Virginia he wrote:

> Indeed I tremble for my country when I reflect that God is just; that his justice cannot sleep forever; that considering numbers, nature and natural means only, a revolution of the wheel of fortune, an exchange of situation is among possible events; that it may become probable by supernatural interference! The Almighty has no attribute which can take side with us in such a contest.

Again, this doesn't sound like a Deist, but someone who believes in God's providence over the nations. While there is debate whether Lincoln was an orthodox Christian, there is no doubt he believed the God of the Bible was directly involved with America and was "the Almighty Ruler of Nations" to the end of "ultimate justice of the people."

Lincoln believed in God's providence prior to the Civil War, but also in the midst of it. After two-and-a-half years of a bloody war, he declared a national holiday of Thanksgiving on October 3, 1863. The proclamation is an inspiring read because it is the opposite of gloom and doom, which so many are given to when all hell breaks loose. The blessings of the bounties America enjoyed, he said, came from the "ever watchful providence of Almighty God." All the many gifts he outlines "are the gracious gifts of the Most High God, who, while dealing with us in anger for our sins, hath nevertheless remembered mercy." I must quote his final words so we can pray that God in our time might raise up leaders who believe as he did, proclaiming:

> [A] day of Thanksgiving and Praise to our beneficent Father who dwelleth in the Heavens. And I recommend to them that while offering up the ascriptions justly due to Him for such singular deliverances and blessings, they do also, with humble penitence for our national perverseness and disobedience, commend to His tender care all those who have become widows, orphans, mourners or sufferers in the lamentable civil strife in which we are unavoidably engaged, and fervently implore the interposition of the Almighty Hand to heal the wounds of the nation and to restore it as soon as may be consistent with the Divine purposes to the full enjoyment of peace, harmony, tranquility and Union.

Belief in the providence of God for most Americans at the time is captured in the well-known hymn, "The Battle Hymn of the Republic." Written in February 1862 by Julia Ward Howe, it originally appeared in the pages of *The Atlantic Monthly*. Howe and her husband were staunch anti-slavery activists, known as abolitionists, and she wrote the song as a pro-Union, anti-slavery anthem to encourage Union troops amid the increasingly bloody civil war.

Things were not looking good for the Union in early 1862. What was expected to be a quick, decisive victory in the defense of the union and against the spread of slavery, turned out to be a brutal bloody slog. Victory for the North was far from assured. As human beings are easily given to predictions of doom, many were sure of the North's demise, which is the context for the hymn. It quickly caught on as the rallying anthem of the Union troops and was sung frequently throughout the rest of the Civil War.

The theme of the hymn proclaims something I fear too many Christians seem to no longer believe in the messy, dysfunctional times in which we live, the triumph of truth. The first stanza boldly declares this:

> Mine eyes have seen the glory of the coming of the Lord:
> He is trampling out the vintage where the grapes of wrath are stored;
> He hath loosed the fateful lightning of His terrible swift sword:
> His truth is marching on.

And the final words declare it again:

> Glory! Glory! Hallelujah! Glory! Glory! Hallelujah!
> Glory! Glory! Hallelujah! His truth is marching on.

Howe was raised in an orthodox Christian Episcopalian home but embraced a Unitarian faith common at the time as she grew into adulthood. However, she penned one of the most popular hymns of the nineteenth century that sounds like it came from a fervent Evangelical. From our perspective we might see her as a nineteenth century "social justice warrior." Her vision, though, wasn't informed by Marxism as it is for the SJW's in our day, but by a Christian worldview common at the time. Regardless of her theology, it was truth and the God of the Bible that drove her, as is apparent in the stirring words of this song.

TRUTH, SECULARISM, AND PROVIDENCE

In a previous chapter, I argued that truth is the dividing line in American culture today, and what Howe teaches us is that you can't separate truth from the God of the Bible. Secularism is the enemy of truth. Without the Bible, or more accurately the God of the Bible, truth doesn't exist. It can't exist. Without God, what makes something "true," or right is the will to power, might makes right. If reality is merely matter then truth has no objective value to the way things are because true north doesn't exist, and there is no need for a compass. If we had one it would have nothing to point to.

As I said in that chapter, Nietzsche believed passionately in truth, but he didn't have the metaphysical justification for truth because of his atheism. You can't get to truth from dirt because if there is no Creator God, all we are is lucky dirt! This is a humungous discussion of epistemology beyond the scope of this book, but America went into a civil war because Americans believe in truth and the God who is the standard of truth. Most in the South believed truth justified enslaving their fellow man, but they still believed it true. The actual truth, however, was on the side of the North because slavery is a moral evil, and it is because of Christianity that we believe this. God's truth was in fact marching on.

British historian Tom Holland wrote a significant book in 2019 called, *Dominion: How the Christian Revolution Remade the Modern World*. A non-Christian, Holland's journey to this conviction is an interesting one. He grew up idolizing the ancient pagan world, but over time realized the assumptions and principles he took for granted about how a society should properly be organized, and the principles that it should uphold—were not bred of classical antiquity, still less of 'human nature', but very distinctively of that civilization's Christian past. So profound has been the impact of Christianity on the development of Western civilization that it has come to be hidden from view.[4] Though hidden, its assumptions and principles are nonetheless Christian, and it is our job to bring them into view. The day of the loud and proud arrogant atheists who proclaimed that "religion poisons everything," in the subtitle of the late Christopher Hitchen's book, *God is Not Great*, is over. A new breed of atheists and agnostics has taken over, and they realize with Nietzsche there is no Western civilization without Christianity.

The Battle Hymn of the Republic was a declaration of the providence of Almighty God which Americans believed well into the twentieth century. As secularism made its march to dominance in the West, God was not so easily discarded. Secularism as a sociological theory predicted that as scientific knowledge increased, religion would "wither on the vine," only it didn't. Even Barack Obama felt the need to leave his church of 20 years when pastor Jeremiah Wright said God should damn America for its racist past, not bless it. Obama knew he would never be president if he didn't distance himself from his pastor who called down curses on America.

A simple internet search will find how American presidents regardless of the depth of their own personal faith, believed God, the Bible, and Christianity are inseparable from America as founded and sustained. In 1911, Woodrow Wilson, the first progressive president, in an address called, "The Bible and Progress" stated this in no uncertain terms:

> The Bible is the one supreme source of revelation of the meaning of life, the nature of God, and spiritual

nature and needs of men. It is the only guide of life which really leads the spirit in the way of peace and salvation. America was born a Christian nation. America was born to exemplify that devotion to the elements of righteousness which are derived from the revelations of Holy Scripture.

Franklin Roosevelt who gave us the New Deal and took the progressive approach to governance to the next level agreed with Wilson:

We cannot read the history of our rise and development as a nation, without reckoning with the place the Bible has occupied in shaping the advances of the Republic. Where we have been the truest and most consistent in obeying its precepts, we have attained the greatest measure of contentment and prosperity.

Roosevelt's successor Harry Truman in a 1950 address stated:

The fundamental basis of this nation's laws was given to Moses on the Mount. The fundamental basis of our Bill of Rights comes from the teachings we get from Exodus and St. Matthew, from Isaiah and St. Paul. I don't think we emphasize that enough these days. If we don't have a proper fundamental moral background, we will finally end up with a totalitarian government which does not believe in rights for anybody except the State!

From 2023 these words appear prophetic. The next president, Dwight Eisenhower, said it even more forcefully:

Without God there could be no American form of government, nor an American way of life. Recognition of the Supreme Being is the first, the most basic, expression of Americanism. Thus, the founding fathers of America saw it, and thus with God's help, it will continue to be.

Jimmy Carter even became president declaring himself a born-again Christian, driven by the conservative Evangelical revival of the 1970s. It wasn't until Barack Obama became president that an occupant of the White House downplayed the Christians character of the nation, even though he identified himself as a practicing Christian. While the state of his soul and the sincerity of his faith is not for me to question, his worldview is of a man of the secular left. In this, he believes America is fundamentally flawed, even if occasionally good, and as we've seen, must be fundamentally transformed. It is to the attempted transformation we now turn.

CHAPTER 5

THE DELUSIONS OF SECULARISM AND OUR MODERN DISCONTENTS

The beginning of Charles Dickens' iconic work, *A Tale of Two Cities*, published in 1859 and set during the French Revolution of the 1790s, could very well describe our own time:

> It was the best of times, it was the worst of times, it was the age of wisdom, it was the age of foolishness, it was the epoch of belief, it was the epoch of incredulity, it was the season of light, it was the season of darkness, it was the spring of hope, it was the winter of despair, we had everything before us, we had nothing before us, we were all going direct to heaven, we were all going direct the other way—in short, the period was so far like the present period, that some of its noisiest authorities insisted on its being received, for good or for evil, in the superlative degree of comparison only.

Until, that is, the blood flowed and heads came off at the behest of the merciful Madame la Guillotine. We'll remember that period became known as "the Reign of Terror."

Despite what many of my fellow Christians might think, I do not believe there is a French Revolution in our present or future. When we compare the two revolutions, we'll see why the American Revolution gives us confidence about a re-founding of America in our time. We all know where we are, and there is no need to catolog the misery. This is a book of hope, not doom, and there is too much of the latter and not enough of the former. But it is important to accurately assess where we are and how we got here so we have a better idea how to fix this mess.

Before we do that, I want to be clear about the claim I'm making. Secularism is dead. It has been weighed on the scales and found wanting. The same applies to its logical offshoot, progressivism, which I'll explore in a subsequent chapter. I believe we are on the other side of secularism, an experiment in Western intellectual and cultural history that isn't turning out quite like its proponents had hoped. After well over a century of cultural dominance, isn't that obvious? It promised everything but delivered nothing but misery and despair. The disaster of secularism was inevitable because it is based on faulty premises and an inaccurate understanding of reality. In other words, it's all a lie, and in the end lies will be revealed for what they are, lies. Truth will always win, sooner or later, because of the One who *is* the Truth. We are, I am convinced, in a time of great awakening, and it's happening all over the world. We must begin with clear eyes and a stout heart, assessing the damage so we know exactly what it is we're fighting.

SECULARISM AND THE SOCIETAL MYTH OF NEUTRALITY

Secularism does its damage on a personal and societal level. Initially it was a response to the Wars of Religion in Europe in the sixteenth and seventeenth centuries. Religion, specifically Christianity, was seen to have dangerous tendencies to promote violence, so in the eighteenth-century Enlightenment thinkers began the slow process of pushing Christianity to the periphery of Western culture. In this telling, Christianity is non-rational, mythological, and prone to violence. Secularism came to the rescue. Embedded in this view of secularism is an assumption we'll call the myth of neutrality, a metaphorically naked public square. Neutral comes from the Latin "neuter" meaning "neither one nor the other," so it's come to mean unbiased which it most certainly is not. In this illusory "neutral" place, secularism is the unbiased referee calling balls and strikes without that pesky Christianity getting involved and inevitably leading to theocracy and intolerance, and thus violence. We'll see how this myth plays out in education in a later chapter, one still accepted by far too many Christians.

Secular, understood classically in the medieval world prior to the Enlightenment, simply meant the mundane as opposed to the sacred. The Reformation rightly critiqued this dichotomy between the secular and the sacred as unbiblical, but the rationalism of Enlightenment thinkers ended up affirming the same dichotomy, only now religion ended up becoming dangerous to social harmony. As Christianity's influence waned in Western civilization, secularism came to dominate the public square as a force hostile to Christianity, and in due course became the dominant worldview of the West. The hostility is expressed in manifold ways throughout government and every area of culture, but there is no need to inventory them here. We're all too depressingly familiar with them as it is.

It is the all-encompassing, tyrannical nature of secularism against which we fight. In their book *Classical Apologetics*, R.C. Sproul, John Gerstner, and Arthur Lindsley start their 1984 book with a chapter titled, "The Crisis of

Secularism." After almost 40 years, that crisis has reached a *revealing* point. Their description of secularism is helpful:

> Western culture is not pagan, nor is it Christian. It has been secularized. Western man has "come of age," passing through the stages of mythology, theology, and metaphysics, reaching the maturity of science. The totem pole has yielded to the temple which in turn has given way to the acme of human progress, the laboratory... Resistance to Christianity comes not from the deposed priests of Isis but from the guns of secularism. The Christian task (more specifically, the rational apologetics task) in the modern epoch is not so much to produce a new *Summa Contra Gentiles* (An apologetics work of Thomas Aquinas to non-Christians) as it is to produce a *Summa Contra Secularisma*.[1]

I could not agree more. The so called "secularization thesis," that as science and knowledge progress religion will eventually disappear, has been completely discredited. The world is arguably more religious than ever, even if the West is less so.

This book embraces that apologetics task, the defense of the Christian faith, against secularism but from a different perspective. Not solely an intellectual or philosophical approach, as critical as those are, it endeavors to make a practical assessment of God's working in history to advance his kingdom and build His church as an apologetic for the Christian faith (see Ephesians 1, specifically verses 21-23). The authors further state the obvious:

> The impact of secularism... has been pervasive and cataclysmic, shaking the foundations of the value

structures of Western civilization. The Judeo-Christian consensus is no more; it has lost its place as the dominant shaping force of cultural ethics... Sooner or later the vacuum (the rejection of theology in the West) will be filled, and if it cannot be filled by the transcendent, then it will be filled by the immanent. The force that floods into such vacuums is statism, the inevitable omega point of secularism.[2]

I could not agree with this more as well, the consequences becoming clearer with every passing year.

SECULARISM AND THE PERSONAL MYTH OF NEUTRALITY: THERE IS NO SUCH THING AS AN UNBELIEVER

On a personal level, the myth of neutrality also does its devious work. It's ubiquitous and easy to spot, but I'll use one example to make the point, a piece from the 2011 print edition of *The New Yorker Magazine* called, "Is That All There Is? Secularism and its discontents." Author James Wood, a committed secularist, admits secularism has its problems, but not enough for him to discard it.

As a secularist, Wood clearly considers himself not "religious," and therefore believes he is neutral regarding ultimate issues. Since he believes he isn't "religious," he also believes he doesn't need faith. The secularist's definition of faith is, however, fallacious and biased, something along the lines of what Samuel Langhorne Clemens, aka Mark Twain, declared, "Faith is believing what you know ain't so." Faith in this view is basically wishful thinking, and not "scientific," as if science could answer metaphysical questions of meaning; it can't. That would be known as a category error. Science and philosophy do different things and address different issues, and most secularists are terrible philosophers. The bias is specifically anti-supernatural because secularists are naturalists or materialists, i.e., they believe the material is all there is. Even if they are not technically philosophical materialists, they are, in fact, every bit as "religious" as the religious.

In other words, the *un*-believer doesn't exist. One of my pet peeves is referring to certain people as believers and others as unbelievers; even Christians do this, all the time. The word believer is biblical, but it's a word we need to retire in our secular age. Using it allows the "unbeliever," the secularist, the false impression they don't have faith just like every "believer." All human beings by the nature of their finite created existence are believers and live by faith; the issue is what or who they believe in. In the apologetics task against secularism, Christians must learn to refer to people either as Christians or non-Christians, not believers and unbelievers.

Throughout the article Wood contrasts religious "believers" with atheists, and at one point refers to "Both atheists and believers..." Ergo, atheists don't have to believe anything! It's almost comical how ridiculous the contrast it. Without the slightest evidence atheists believe all material reality basically created itself, everything came from nothing. Talk about a leap of faith! Wood might even say he doesn't need the "crutch" of faith like many atheists, but atheism and secularism are a rickety crutch. You'll see throughout his piece something else secularists are especially good at, begging the question, a logical fallacy meaning to assume the premise as the conclusion, a form of circular reasoning. A great example of this is early in the piece when he lays his cards on the table claiming, "God is dead, and cannot be reimposed on existence." The bald assertion is never defended, just asserted, as if it need not be defended; but it is a statement of faith. We must question the unexamined assumptions of the secularist *and* secularism wherever they rear their ugly head.

C.S. Lewis said something that underlies the impossibility of neutrality in the Christian understanding of reality:

> There is no neutral ground in the universe: every square inch, every split second, is claimed by God and counterclaimed by Satan.[3]

In other words, there is a spiritual war being waged on the vast plane of reality, and only one side wins.

MAKING THE SECULAR PLAUSIBLE

I introduced the concept of plausibility structures in the first chapter, the idea that society is a structure of the plausible, what *seems* real and natural and normal to us—just the way things are. The truth of the seeming is irrelevant. We'll see how a turn to the subjective in Western intellectual history enabled a complete inversion of how people view the world and led to horrible consequences. Our focus for the moment, however, is the worldview of those who inhabit this secular plausibility structure. I will reiterate what I said in the first chapter: we are all susceptible to the lies and illusions of a secular view of reality, so it's especially important to understand them.

James K.A. Smith in his book summarizing the magisterial tome of Canadian philosopher Charles Taylor, *A Secular Age*, entitled his book, *How (Not) to be Secular*. He has numerous helpful insights into the nature of secularism. In speaking of plausibility, he mentions Taylor's "conditions of belief," saying there was "a shift in the plausibility conditions that make something believable or unbelievable." It's not so much what people believe, as what is believable. These are reflected in "the default assumptions" of a people. These ideas are unexamined and taken for granted by everyone, and thus most secular people don't think they assume anything at all. Commenting on these "conditions of belief," Smith gives us a helpful perspective on the implications for faith:

> Taylor not only explains *un*belief in a secular age; he also emphasizes that even belief is changed in our secular age. There are still believers who believe the same things as their forebearers 1,500 years ago; but *how* we believe has changed. Thus faith communities need to ask: How does this change in the "conditions" of belief impact the way we proclaim and teach the faith? How does this impact faith formation? How should this change the propagation of the faith for the next generation?[4]

Even though Smith makes my previous point referring to believers when the whole paragraph is about belief, he does say later, "[I]t's not that our secular age is an age of *dis*belief; it's an age of believing otherwise."[5] And in this sense, everyone is a believer.

In simplest terms, secularism means "no God." It doesn't necessitate atheistic materialism, although all atheists are secularists. Rather, God is persona non grata, unwelcome at the dinner table whether he exists or not. Since atheists are few and far between, most people in the West are not unlike ancient Epicureans who believed the gods existed but thought they had no relevance to life. Secularists are fundamentally, if not philosophically, materialists because the only thing that really matters to them is the material world; flourishing in this world is all that counts. An irrelevant God is the secular cultural air we breathe, and the dominant cultural messaging, which is why the personal and societal effects of secularism are ubiquitous and profound.

The dominant modern Epicurean secularist faith is something called moralistic therapeutic Deism (TDS), a phrase sociologists Christian Smith and Melinda Lundquist Denton coined in their 2005 book *Soul Searching: The Religious and Spiritual Lives of American Teenagers*. As they lay it out in the book such people believe:

1. A God exists who created and ordered the world and watches over human life on earth.
2. God wants people to be good, nice, and fair to each other, as taught in the Bible and by most world religions.
3. The central goal of life is to be happy and to feel good about oneself.
4. God does not need to be particularly involved in one's life except when God is needed to resolve a problem.
5. Good people go to heaven when they die.[6]

This god is no threat to secularism because it is a religion of secularism. Also, like Epicureanism, while both ancients and moderns believe gods or God exist, they both have no need to obsess over death. The ancient Epicureans got rid of the fear of death by asserting that we cease to exist when we die, whereas the modern Epicureans figure if we're decent people we go heaven when we die, so no need to worry about it. What's important is the here and now. Why worry about all that stuff we really can't know, and everyone disagrees with anyway?

SECULARISM AND THE TURN TO THE SUBJECTIVE

The most consequential turn to secularism of Christian Western civilization is related to ontology, or the study of being. The empiricism of Bacon and the rationalism of Descartes made epistemology, or the study of knowing, the focus of Western intellectual debate, relegating ontology to an afterthought. Once the starting point of philosophy became man and knowing, not God and being, it was only a matter of time before man would seriously believe the temptation of satan, that he could "be like God, knowing good and evil." This revolution in Western thought turned from God being the object, then man in relation to Him, to the entire cosmos solely being anthropocentric, about man.

There are various ways this manifests itself and can be explained. Smith taking from Taylor, says the disenchantment of the "buffered" modern self

> is primarily a shift in the *location* of meaning, moving it from "the world" *into* "the mind." Significance no longer inheres in things; rather meaning and significance are a property of minds who perceive meaning internally... Meaning is now located in *agents*.[7]

Taylor in his book *The Malaise of Modernity*, conveys this absorption of the self in numerous ways, one of which is authenticity. Going back to the original bohemian eighteenth century philosopher Jean Jacques Rousseau, he explains:

> Self-determining freedom is in part the default solution of the culture of authenticity, while at the same time it is its bane, since it further intensifies

75

anthropocentrism. This sets up a vicious circle that heads us toward a point where our major remaining value is choice itself.[8]

Ah, choice, the holy grail of modern existence.

Alasdair MacIntyre in his book, *After Virtue*, calls this move to the subjective emotivism:

> Emotivism is the doctrine that all evaluative judgments and more specifically all moral judgments are nothing but expressions of preference, expressions of attitude or feelings, insofar as they are moral or evaluative in character... Emotivism has become embodied in our culture.[9]

For most people right and wrong are basically preferences like what flavor of ice cream one prefers. But bring up the Holocaust and they aren't so eager to carry the analogy that far. If secularism is true, though, genocide is not objectively morally evil. You say tom-A-to, I say tom-ah-to.

Another explanation of how this turn to the subjective works itself out can be found in the work of sociologist Philip Rieff (1922–2006). Although he was a secular Jew, he saw more presciently than most the futility of trying to maintain Western civilization without Christianity. The title of his most famous work says it all, *The Triumph of the Therapeutic*. We saw above how the therapeutic is central to the religious faith of most secular Westerners; what's in it for me, what makes me feel good, makes me happy. That is their religion. Reiff saw prophetically where this would lead:

> We believe that we know something our predecessors did not: that we can live feely at last, enjoying all our

senses—except the sense of the past—as unremember-
ing, honest, and friendly barbarians, in a technological
Eden... In our recovered innocence, to be entertained
would become the highest good and boredom the most
common evil... The best spirits of the twentieth century
have thus expressed their conviction that the original
innocence, which to earlier periods was a sinful conceit,
the new center, which can be held even as communities
disintegrate, is the self. By this conviction a new and
dynamic acceptance of disorder, in love with life and
destructive of it, has been loosed upon the world.[10]

Looking back on these words from the third decade of
the twenty first century, it is easy to see how prophetic Rieff
was, comparable to Nietzsche at the end of the previous
century who predicted the "death of God" would unleash the
horrors of the twentieth century.

THE SECULAR TURN TO THE SUBJECTIVE REVEALS
THE OBJECTIVE NATURE OF REALITY

If my contention that we're on the other side of secularism
is accurate, the question is why. What is it about where we
are now that is allowing the true nature of secularism to be
revealed? As I said above secularism is a spent force, which
means it's being revealed as the hollow malignancy it has
always been. We are in a moment of great revealing when
things that should have been obvious all along are starting
to become undeniably obvious to an increasing number of
people on both a societal and personal level.

Subjectivism is inevitably self-defeating and can't be
consistent with its own premises. It's like saying there are
no such thing as absolutes, and that is absolutely true! Such

an assertion is as absurd as the English sentence, there are no sentences in English. What exactly is the premise of secularism? It can be traced back to when man succumbed to Satan's temptation that he could be like God, which is the essence of the turn to the subjective. The first commandment is that we shall have no other gods before us, but ever since the Garden we want to call the shots. The first commandment makes it very clear; we don't get to do that. When we try, or think we can, misery and destruction are not far behind. Objective reality, the created order as God made it, will never cooperate with the usurper.

Because we live in God's cause and effect universe, human beings reap what they sow on a societal or personal level. That is why secularism regardless of how or where it is manifested is ultimately self-defeating, no matter what it looks like at the moment. Although this fragility doesn't appear that way to most people now, to make this point I often use the analogy of the Berlin Wall, once a symbol of the apparent permanence of Soviet communism.

I was only one year old when construction on the wall began, and as I grew up it was a Cold War feature of life, part of the furniture of a world that included a Soviet Union. I became politically aware in my 20s, and like everyone else I expected the Berlin Wall to be as enduring as the Soviet Union itself. Then Ronald Reagan, God bless him, seemed to have a different assessment of the situation. In his first press conference after he was elected president, Reagan stated that no Soviet leader had ever abandoned the quest for worldwide communist domination. He was willing to say what must not be said. The foreign policy establishment was committed to something called "containment," which meant keeping communism within certain bounds. The Soviet leaders were obviously not informed about containment.

In a March 1983 speech, he denounced the Soviet Union as "an evil empire" and "the focus of evil in the modern world." Now Ronnie had really gone off the rails. Asked about his Cold War strategy early in his presidency, he replied, "We win, they lose." Official Washington called him a warmonger, a cowboy, a loose cannon who was going to get us into a nuclear war, but ignoring the critics and all the "experts," he developed a plan to win. Speaking against the policy of containment in 1981 at Notre Dame University, Reagan said:

> The West will not contain communism; it will tran-scend communism. We will not bother to renounce it; we'll dismiss it as a bizarre chapter in human history whose last pages are even now being written.

Liberal politicians and the media establishment mocked Reagan for saying such things, but he knew reality can-not be mocked forever. Everything about communism flies in the face of God's creational order, even as secularism and woke leftism do today. In a speech he gave before the British Parliament at Westminster Palace on June 8, 1982, he argued reality would win. Among those arguments was "Regimes planted by bayonets do not take root . . ." Nor do regimes in America that stifle free speech or weaponize law enforcement against their political enemies. He realized what very few at the time did, "It may not be easy to see; but I believe we live now at a turning point." I believe we are now in a similar turning point regarding secularism, and for similar reasons: A government that rejects God and crushes human freedom and dignity cannot last. Then Reagan delivered one of the most mocked lines of all as he continued:

What I am describing now is a plan and a hope for the long term—the march of freedom and democracy which will leave Marxism-Leninism on the ash-heap of history, as it has left other tyrannies which stifle the freedom and muzzle the self-expression of the people.

Less than 10 years later, the Soviet Union was gone, smoldering on the ash-heap of history just as he predicted.

SECULARISM, ALEKSANDR SOLZHENITSYN, AND OUR BERLIN WALL

In June 1987 Reagan gave probably his most famous speech standing before the Berlin Wall. Nobody in his administration or the foreign policy establishment thought he should utter the most legendary line in the speech: "Mr. Gorbachev, tear down this wall!" It just wasn't polite! Ronnie didn't care. But I, along with about 99.99% of the world, thought that might be a nice wish, but it's not happening, at least in our lifetimes. It's impossible to fathom unless you lived through it and were politically and culturally engaged what a pipe dream this appeared to be.

I often get the same kind of response when I declare secularism in our day is as enduring as the Berlin Wall. It is based on the exact same reality mocking ideas that animated Soviet communism for its 70-year existence, and like the Berlin Wall secularism is coming down. All of this was apparent for the entire 70 years, but only Reagan and a few others seemed to grasp the revelatory nature of communism's failures. The exact same failures of secularism are happening all around us, if only we have eyes to see the revealing.

One who did at the time was Russian dissident, novelist, and historian, Aleksandr Solzhenitsyn. In an address accepting the Templeton Prize for Progress in Religion in 1983, he identified the fundamental issue of our time. Speaking to the death and destruction wrought by communism in Russia in the twentieth century "that swallowed up some 60 million of our people," he said he "could not put it more accurately than to repeat: 'Men have forgotten God; that's why all this happened.'" He used phrases like, "deprived of its divine dimensions..." and "lacking all divine dimensions..." and "our Godless age..." and "The entire twentieth century is being sucked into the vortex of atheism and self-destruction."

A better description of secularism could not be found, "Men have forgotten God... " Speaking of Russian history in the same address he said:

> Russia felt the first whiff of secularism; its subtle poisons permeated the educated classes in the course of the nineteenth century and opened the path to Marxism. By the time of the Revolution, faith had virtually disappeared in Russian educated circles; and amongst the uneducated, its health was threatened.

Later in the talk he spoke of "the destructive spirit of secularism." Destructive indeed. Solzhenitsyn tended to pessimism, but who could blame him given what he went through. He continued identifying the need of our age if we're to defeat secularism as the reigning orthodoxy of our time:

> No-one expects the Churches to merge or to revise all their doctrines, but only to present a common front

against atheism. But for such a purpose the steps taken are much too slow.

We might wonder how he'd feel looking back forty years later, but he'd likely be even more pessimistic. As we'll see, I believe we don't need to be pessimistic because "the destructive spirit of secularism" needs to play itself out much as Soviet communism did, to reveal its deep-seated bankruptcy. In no way imaginable can it deliver what it promises, and that becomes clearer to more people every day. Now is our opportunity.

I very much like his prudent suggestion, that even though churches need not revise their doctrines, they must present a common front against, in this case, secularism. In my four-plus decades as a Christian it is disconcerting how much time Christians spend in internecine warfare. Sound doctrine is important, critical in fact, but other Nicene Christians are not the enemy—secularism is. God in his wisdom didn't see fit to give us an exhaustive theological textbook, therefore there will always be plenty of disagreement. However, Christians of every tradition can agree on what C.S. Lewis wrote so eloquently and forcefully, "*Mere Christianity.*" It is the Nicaean tradition of Trinitarian faith rooted in Scripture that stands as the bulwark of Christian Western Civilization and the foundation for the evangelization of the world. Even though Christianity's influence in Western culture gave us secularism, it stands now as the implacable foe of everything Christian *and* civilization and must be unmasked for what it is.

Now that we've identified the enemy, my specific theological convictions and Christian worldview will inform the arguments I make in the coming chapters related to my political philosophy and vision for the future. I trust they will be narrowly broad enough to appeal to "mere Christians," and to non-Christians as well who understand how Christian Western civilization came from the deep well of the death, burial, and resurrection of Christ, and those who followed in its wake.

CHAPTER 6

MARXISM,
THE LIE THAT WILL NOT DIE

Most Americans know little about Marxism, or that it is responsible for Western culture going woke. It is critical we understand Marxism so we can expose its fundamental fraudulence. My basic contention is the same about Marxism as it was about secularism. Marxism is dead, obviously in its traditional "orthodox" form, but also dying in its "new and improved" cultural form known as wokeness. Like secularism, it too is a spent force. I know this will be counterintuitive to almost all my readers who will rightly point out that cultural Marxism in the form of wokeness is at the pinnacle of its influence in the West and controls almost all governments, the cultures that sustain them, and their partners in the globalist corporate elite.

My argument is that it must be at its pinnacle of influence to be exposed for what it is, evil from the pit of hell. As the evil is unmasked, people who have been red-pilled will be more open to the author of truth who is the Truth. Therefore, the great revealing happening in our day is ultimately evangelical for the advancing of God's kingdom and building of Christ's church. The evangelical nature of this revealing is happening because Christianity claims to be the ultimate explanation for the nature of reality, and reality is fighting back and debunking the lies of secularism and Marxism. Jesus said Satan is the father of lies, and when he lies, he speaks his native language. Satan's lying deception has one purpose: to destroy God's greatest creation, man, and it started with his greatest lie in Genesis 3, that man could be "like God knowing good and evil." That hasn't worked out so well, and the more his lies succeed and work themselves out in history, the more apparent it becomes they are in fact lies and ultimately unsustainable.

The reason lies never ultimately win comes from God's revelation in creation: "In the beginning God created the heavens and the earth" (Gen. 1:1). Creation, what some call nature, works in certain ways because God made it to work that way. To the contrary, as James Lindsay puts it, the transforming of reality is "the essential Marxist project."[1] But because it is in fact true that reality is God created, and He is merciful and gracious, what's happening in our time is that the created nature of reality is asserting itself. Noelle Mering puts this wonderfully:

> The very nature of God implies an intelligible moral order to the universe, an order which, though we might deny it, is akin to the denial of gravity. We might be free falling for a time, but at some point, the spiritual physics will cause us to confront the ground.[2]

Boom! Splattered shattered body. That person can deny gravity all the way down until... that's the way the reveal happens... Boom! Splattered shattered reality, death of an old worldview, a new one being born, resurrected from the ashes. Created reality reveals itself and illusions die in what is often a slow, painful death. This happens to individuals, of course, but it also happens to societies and civilizations because they are filled with human beings made in God's image. We are, I believe, in a civilizational worldview transition, and only God knows how it will come to His desired end. To continue this journey, we must explore the most influential perversion of reality ever to infect the mind of sinful man, Marxism.

MARXISM PROVES SATAN IS A DIABOLICAL GENIUS

For a failed philosophy, Marxism just won't die. Fortunately, at its most powerful in a form Karl Marx wouldn't recognize but would cheer nonetheless, it's revealing itself to be the impotent failure it has always been. Unfortunately, prior to being laid in the coffin, it leaves massive amounts of misery, suffering, and death in its wake as we've witnessed since October 1917. Marxism has morphed and shape-shifted over time like the T-1000 cyborg in *Terminator 2*, and like T-1000 it remains the same essence: a malevolent philosophy creating misery and havoc wherever it goes, all in the name of perpetual revolution and an undefinable Utopia.

We now understand Marxism in a way we never could before its current cultural manifestations, and why it's an enemy far more pernicious and insidious in its present cultural form than it ever was in its orthodox Karl Marx economic class-based form. That's a staggering claim given north of one hundred million(!) people were butchered in the name of Marx's communism in the twentieth century. Before we get to the current perversion in its cultural manifestations, it is important to understand the basics of its orthodox version in the mind of Marx. Even the "orthodox" form wasn't real Marxism because true Marxism was a theoretical illusion in the minds of Karl Marx (1818-1883) and Friedrich Engels (1820-1895), his collaborator who funded

Marx's life's work. Both men dreamed of a Utopia, an imaginary and ideal place where all suffering and misery caused by capitalism would fade away to endless Nirvana.

The reason I focus on the devil in a chapter on Marxism is because the deeper you dive down into this Hegelian-Marxist Wonderland rabbit hole, the more you realize the diabolical is the *only* explanation that can make sense of the nightmare of Marxism in both its economic and cultural forms. In our secular, desacralized age, the devil is often portrayed as a benign if malevolent figure in a red suit with horns and a tail, a character in a play. He is anything but.

In *The Screwtape Letters,* C.S. Lewis has the senior demon tell his protégé it is policy to keep his subject ignorant of his presence. He proceeds to tell him that's easy to do:

> The fact that 'devils' are predominantly comic figures in the modern imagination will help you. If any faint suspicion in your existence begins to arise in his mind, suggest to him a picture of something in red tights, and persuade him that since he cannot believe in that (it is an old textbook method of confusing them) he therefore cannot believe in you.[3]

Lewis says that's one error people fall into regarding the devil. "The other is to believe and to feel an excessive and unhealthy interest in them."[4] Lewis died before the 1973 hit movie *The Exorcist* which ushered in a popular culture of "unhealthy interest" in the demonic, making the actual devil no more believable to secular people than the comic portrayal. That terrifying devil doesn't show up in their lived experience any more than the comic one, so he can't be real.

In the first chapter I wrote about Naomi Wolf coming to believe in God again because of what she perceived in the response to Covid, "the very impressiveness of evil all around us in all of its awful majesty." She said:

> It was so cruel, an almost superhuman flamboyant, baroque imagination made from the essence of cruelty itself, that I could not conceive that it had been accomplished by mere humans working on the bumbling human level in the dumb political space.[5]

I feel the same way learning about both Georg Wilhelm Friedrich Hegel and Karl Marx turning his thought into Marxism. The exquisite evil gets even more impressive in light of the failure of orthodox Marxism, and other evil geniuses transforming it into cultural Marxism.

HEGEL AND THE DIALECTIC

We can't understand Marx or Marxism in its various malevolent manifestations without some understanding of Hegel's philosophy.[6] To dive in too deeply is mind numbing, but thankfully, unnecessary. Even a cursory understanding demonstrates when a man, or a culture, rejects God's revelation in Scripture, the flights of fancy can reach unimaginable perversity. The fallen human mind left to speculation has an almost infinite capacity for such intellectual perversion which always leads to misery and suffering.

It is important, however, to be fair to Hegel because he believed himself to be a Christian defending Christianity in the age of Enlightenment skepticism. And I take it from others and what I've read of him, that it's rarely easy to decipher what he meant. Having rejected biblical revelation, his speculations were bound to end up in a place he didn't intend, and Marx ensured that they did. Hegel's thinking had two lines of interpretation, one conservative and the other radical, the latter known as "the young Hegelians," among those being Marx himself. The most vocal of the radicals were atheists who hijacked Hegel's dialectic in the name of atheistic materialism, which in due course came to be known as dialectical materialism.

To get philosophical for a moment, Hegel saw God as the world spirit in history, the Absolute, with its apotheosis in the state. In other words, the ideal of this world spirit's self-realization is in the state. This process is driven by the dialectic, a concept he got from Kant and another German philosopher, Johann Gottlieb Fichte (1762-1814). History has its own inner necessity, an inevitability, all realized and revealed through this dialectical historical process. Whatever exists in this historical cultural moment, the "zeitgeist" or "spirt of the age," is the thesis, which has its own internal inconsistencies and problems and must be critiqued. This in turn creates its antithesis, and through human reason grappling with these two opposites, the new thesis will emerge, and so on to its ultimate realization. Paul Kengor writes:

> Some Hegel scholars believe that Hegel's interpretation of the resurrection of Jesus Christ on the final day is the actual conclusion of the march and movement of history that Hegel expected.[7]

The young Hegelians would have none of that. In fact, the young Hegelians thought Hegel was too religious, and wrote critiques of various aspects of his philosophy. Marx wrote approvingly of another young Hegelian, Ludwig Feuerbach (1804-1872):

Feuerbach is the only one who has a serious, critical attitude to the Hegelian dialectic and who has made genuine discoveries in this field. He is in fact the true conqueror of the old philosophy. The extent of his achievement, and the unpretentious simplicity with which he, Feuerbach, gives it to the world, stand in striking contrast to the opposite attitude [of the others].[8]

In Marx's purview, the young Hegelians won the day.

CLASS OPPRESSION AND THE FOUNDATIONS OF "ORTHODOX" MARXISM

When I was 24, the man who would become my intellectual and theological mentor said we need to take Marx seriously because he obviously appealed to many people, and we should try to understand that appeal. This is more critical today than ever. That was in the mid-1980s when cultural Marxism was only starting to infect higher education and orthodox, class-based Marxism had a little remaining credibility. The Soviet Union still existed, the Berlin Wall still stood, and most everyone (including me) except for Ronald Reagan and a few others thought both would last beyond our lifetimes. Its demise fooled many of us into believing Marxism itself was on the ash-heap of history, not just the Soviet version.

The communism of Marx didn't come out of the void but was part of the intellectual stew bubbling up throughout Europe in response to the economic suffering of the industrial revolution. People, especially intellectuals, were looking for answers to the misery brought on by the many great changes happening in the nineteenth century. The appeal has a certain plausibility based on something sinful human beings are never in short supply of, envy.

The great enemy in Marx's vision is the bourgeoisie, or the middle class, the owners of capital. The victims are the working class or the proletariat. In a typical passage about this conflict from his *Communist Manifesto*, Marx explains the dynamic that justifies communism:

> In proportion as the bourgeoisie, i.e., capital, is developed, in the same proportion is the proletariat, the modern working class, developed—a class of laborers, who live only so long as they find work, and who find work only so long as their labor increases capital. These laborers, who must sell themselves piecemeal, are a commodity, like every other article of commerce . . .[9]

When people become a commodity, according to Marx, they are alienated from themselves, others, and society itself. On the metaphysical level of this struggle, alienation is at the core of Marx's religion, which he and Marxists would deny was a religion, but it has all the hallmarks of one. In fact, many have called Marxism a Christian heresy because it has a creation narrative, Darwinism, a fall, capitalism, sin, private property, redemption through blood, revolution, and eschatology, the inevitable Utopia of a classless society. Robert M. Smith in an article on cultural Marxism explains this well:

> Alasdair MacIntyre once described Marxism as "a secularism formed by the gospel which is committed to the problem of power and justice and therefore to themes of redemption and renewal." The problem,

however, is that its diagnosis is superficial, and its cure fatal. For this reason, Marxism, whether in classical or cultural form, can be viewed as a corruption or parody of the gospel—replete with its own false prophet (Marx), false Bible (Das Kapital), false doctrine (dialectical materialism), false apostles (Lenin, Stalin, Mao, Marcuse), and false hope (a communist utopia). Therefore, the fact that Cultural Marxism is a real ideology making a real impact on our world is not good news.[10]

The Metaphysical seduction is the purported alienation. Man, according to Marx, puts his essence, his being into the work of his hands. The idea of the ultimate, almost spiritual value of manual labor is why the hammer and sickle on communist flags represents the proletariat or the common man, the laborer. If he is paid wages he is then alienated from his creation, and thus himself, and everything else.

Here is a quote from Herbert Marcuse (1898-1979) describing how this process of alienation happens:

> Marx's writings between 1844 and 1846 treat the form of labor in modern society as constituting the total 'alienation' of man. The employment of this category links Marx's economic analysis with a basic category of the Hegelian philosophy. The social division of labor, Marx declares, is not carried out with any consideration for the talents of individuals and the interest of the whole, but rather takes place entirely according to the laws of capitalist commodity production. Under these laws, the product of labor, the commodity, seems to determine the nature and end of human activity. In other words, the materials

that should serve life come to rule over its content and goal, and the consciousness of man is completely made victim to the relationships of material production.[11]

Man is oppressed by "modern society" and "capitalist commodity production," therefore man is victim and life is a perpetual power dynamic of the oppressor, the capitalist, against the oppressed, the proletariat. Marx says the latter are enslaved, and their condition a despotism. He starts his Manifesto with:

> The history of all hitherto existing society is the history of class struggles... oppressor and oppressed ... in constant opposition to one another.[12]

It won't surprise us that the man who saw existence in such miserable terms was himself a miserable human being. Paul Kengor in his book *The Devil and Karl Marx* states about this miserable man:

> Marxism's founder was a seriously perverse man who brooded in misery, wallowed in misery, advanced himself in the name of misery, and ultimately produced misery.[13]

Looking back at the last hundred plus years, who can deny that final assertion. This initial version of Marxism was primarily economic, and class based, until it failed and required a reboot in its current cultural form which broadened the oppression from the realm of economics to the entire culture. From the grave, Marx has been able to spread the misery.

MARX'S WORLDVIEW AND HIS ENEMIES

It isn't news that Marxism is radical, but for many people Marxism and communism (and socialism) are just words without much in the way of content. Engels in his preface to the *Manifesto* describes "the history of the modern working-class movement," and declares just how radical communism needs to be because of the "insufficiency of mere political revolutions." What is needed is "a total social change."[14] There can be no tinkering around the edges if there is going to be true societal transformation. Marx puts it bluntly:

> The Communist revolution is the most radical rupture with traditional property relations; no wonder that its development involved the most radical rupture with traditional ideas.[15]

If we're going to understand this rupture of Marxism as it's come to us in cultural form, we need to understand those traditional ideas standing in the way of Marx's perpetual revolution. These are the most important on his enemies' list:

1. Private property
2. The family
3. The nation-state
4. Religion, i.e., Christianity

Let's explore why. A person's theology determines his anthropology. In other words, what we think about God determines our understanding of man, and this applies to atheists like Marx as much as Christians and other theists. From this follows that every religion and philosophy has a theodicy, from Greek theos, "god" and dikē, "justice", and addresses the problem of evil and why it exists. Even without God evil must be accounted for in some way, and must be justified. Thus, the perennial question echoing in every human heart throughout history is *why*? Nobody is satisfied with *just because*.

Therefore, to explain the horrors of life somehow, Marx took his cue from the anthropology of Rousseau who asserted his belief in the innate goodness of man in the first words of his book, *The Social Contract*: "Man is born free, but everywhere he is in chains." Out of Rousseau's writing the idea of the noble savage, an ancient concept, gained traction in the Romantic movement of the eighteenth and nineteenth centuries. As a materialist with no concept of original sin, Marx believed man was basically good. It was society in the form of capitalism that corrupted man and made him the perpetual victim of his oppressors.

This perspective on human nature completely eviscerates personal responsibility and human agency, making victimization the driver of human existence. No wonder those programmed into this worldview (primarily via education and culture) are so miserable. That, as we'll see, is the point; only miserable people are ripe for revolution.

PRIVATE PROPERTY

The idea of human beings owning property is foundational to a well-ordered society with maximal liberty. Those who are not allowed to own property, as in communism, are no better off than slaves who can't own property but are in fact the property of others. There is no direct affirmation of "private property" in the Bible, but it is everywhere assumed. The word property is common, used 50 to 60 times in the Old Testament (depending on the translation). The Hebrew word means possession. What a person possesses they own; it is their property. This is codified in the Ten Commandments in what is called "the second table of the law," or six through ten. Most directly it is in the command that we shall not steal, which assume others' property or possessions belong to them. The Lord makes the point even more powerfully in the tenth commandment against coveting, meaning we are not even to desire anything anyone else calls their own.

Contrary to the entire biblical witness, Marx is unequivocal in his antipathy to private property:

> In this sense, the theory of the Communists may be summed up in the single sentence: Abolition of private property.[16]

He does qualify this abolition with "in this sense" referring to the Edenic paradise prior to "the fall," and before man the noble savage was corrupted:

> Do you mean the property of the petty artisan and of the small peasant, a form of property that preceded the bourgeois form? There is no need to abolish that; the development of industry has to a great extent already destroyed it, and is still destroying it daily. Or do you mean modern bourgeois private property? But does wage-labor create any property for the laborer? Not a bit. It creates capital, i.e., that kind of property which exploits wage-labor, and which cannot increase except upon condition of begetting a new supply of wage-labor for fresh exploitation.[17]

MARXISM, THE LIE THAT WILL NOT DIE

In other words, to Marx real private property which is truly (spiritually, ontologically) owned by the person in "modern society" and "capitalist commodity production" cannot exist. Anything called private property in such a society, the only one that exists, must be "abolished" because it leads to "fresh exploitation."

THE FAMILY

As Christians, we don't need to establish the biblical basis for the family, but we do need to argue that the family, once commonly referred to as the nuclear family, i.e., father, mother, children, is the natural order of things. Every society in world history developed with the family as the fundamental building block of its civilization. Even those cultures that practiced polygamy required the man's commitment to his spouses and children. Through families a culture's moral values and framework are passed on from generation to generation, and as such must be destroyed by communists. A society comprised primarily of families will never be ripe for revolution or develop the necessary revolutionary consciousness in the population. Marx is also unequivocal about this:

> Abolition of the family! Even the most radical flare up at this infamous proposal of the communists. On what foundation is the present family, the bourgeois family, based? On capital, on private gain. In its completely developed form this family exists only among the bourgeoisie.[18]

Like with most of Marx's assertions, he begs the question, assuming any family in "modern society" and "capitalist commodity production" is not in fact a "family." Therefore, such "families" must be abolished. As with everything else in the Marxist philosophy, this is supposed to happen naturally as dialectical materialism works itself out in history:

> The bourgeois family will vanish as a matter of course when its compliment vanishes, and both will vanish with the vanishing of capital.[19]

As we witnessed in the twentieth century, nothing vanishes "as a matter of course," which is why communist regimes are always tyrannical, totalitarian, and bloody.

Marx also addresses education because that can't be allowed to perpetuate the bourgeois family. Therefore, education must be rescued "from the influence of the ruling class," and "home education" replaced by "social education."[20] This didn't work at all in Marx's economic model of communism but has worked brilliantly in the culture version as we'll see in the chapter on the Marxification of Education.

THE NATION STATE

It was the gospel, the good news, given to us in Christ, and expanded to the Gentiles by the Apostle Paul that made Christianity the only universal religion on earth. However, since Christianity isn't Utopian the idea of a borderless world never took hold among Christians. It is, however, a requirement for communists. There must be no hierarchy or authority because all such things, including the nation state, will vanish in the inexorable development of history.

As with his critics' take on private property and the family, Marx addresses those who bring up this criticism, "The Communists are further reproached with desiring to abolish countries and nationality." His reply? "The workingmen have no country."[21] So, just like property and family, which by Marxist definition can't exist in a bourgeois society, neither can "countries and nationality." This is yet another reason why Christianity was and is the implacable foe of Marxism because it stands in their way. This includes the modern nation-state which developed in Christian Western civilization in many ways because of its Jewish and Christian roots. The idea of nations or peoples is ubiquitous in the Bible, so it stands as a fundamental bulwark to the universalist pretensions of the Marxists as well as the modern globalists who are their offspring.

RELIGION, I.E., CHRISTIANITY

Here we come to the crux of the matter. Marx knew it was either Christianity or communism; neither could exist in the same world. He never saw the need to argue for or in any way try to prove his atheism. Like many Enlightenment and post-Enlightenment thinkers, it was too obvious to bother. Everything in Marx's philosophy flowed from his anti-Christian animus. Even though the cultural Marxists believed Marx was in error about economics being the driver of revolution, they embraced this central aspect of Marx's worldview, that hostility to Christianity would make perpetual revolution possible.

Religion, by which Marx always means Christianity, gets the same treatment as every other "traditional idea." It is dismissed as historically conditioned oppression. His most famous take on religion, or infamous depending on one's perspective, is not in the *Manifesto*, but in his "Critique of Hegel's Philosophy of Right":

> Religious suffering is, at one and the same time, the expression of real suffering and a protest against real

suffering. Religion is the sight of the oppressed creature, the heart of a heartless world, and the soul of
soulless conditions. It is the opium of the people.

The abolition of religion as the illusory happiness
of the people is the demand for their real happiness.
To call on them to give up their illusions about their
condition is to call on them to give up a condition that
requires illusions...

The criticism of religion disillusions man, so that
he will think, act, and fashion his reality like a man
who has discarded his illusions and regained his
senses, so that he will move around himself as his
own true Sun. Religion is only the illusory Sun which
revolves around man as long as he does not revolve
around himself.[22]

His criticism of religion is tinged with a contrived concern for people who supposedly suffer from oppression and
look to an illusion to dull the pain. These people may think
they are happy, but that too is an illusion keeping them
from real happiness. You have to hand it to the guy. Here is
a miserable man selling happiness to people who by definition will always be miserable (it's a requirement) until the
revolution brings everything to the dialectical end of history.
And people bought it! And still do.

The satanic core at the heart of Marxism is blatant: man
must be his own God, he must "revolve around himself."
John Lennon, who was no Marxist (he left England to live
in New York to escape the confiscatory taxation) penned
an ode to communism that couldn't be said any better by
Marx himself:

Imagine there's no heaven
It's easy if you try
No hell below us
Above us only sky
Imagine all the people
Living for today... Aha-ah...

Imagine there's no countries
It isn't hard to do
Nothing to kill or die for
And no religion, too
Imagine all the people
Living life in peace... You...

Imagine no possessions
I wonder if you can
No need for greed or hunger
A brotherhood of man
Imagine all the people
Sharing all the world... You...

You may say I'm a dreamer
But I'm not the only one
I hope someday you'll join us
And the world will live as one.

We don't have to imagine what such a world would look like. The evidence of death, misery, and destruction are apparent for all with eyes to see, to see. The cultural Marxists don't have such eyes, and we'll now see how Marx's failure paved the way for his ultimate success in cultural Marxism.

CHAPTER 7

THE BIRTH OF CULTURAL MARXISM AND WOKENESS

As we saw, Marx's communism wasn't so inevitable after all; it didn't turn out anything like he or his acolytes thought it would. Capitalist societies were supposed to fall to the inevitable revolution of the proletariat, but material comforts were more appealing than the promise of an abstract communist Utopia. And the only revolution that did happen was in the least industrial society, Russia, and from a top-down oligarchy not the bottom up like Marx predicted. Calling it communism couldn't mask the failure, and doctrinaire Marxists knew it. And even though a version of Marxism supposedly took hold in Russia, these Marxists knew it wasn't the transformation of the world they were looking for. Marxists, though, weren't willing to give up on their Marxism and something had to change; thus was born cultural Marxism.

THE FRANKFURT SCHOOL

The primary insight of the cultural Marxists wasn't that class-based economic oppression didn't bring the fruit of revolution Marx promised, but that the revolutionary consciousness required clearly would not arise spontaneously;

it must be assiduously cultivated via culture. They recognized Western societies produced cultures that were almost completely resistant to revolution. Marxist revolutionary consciousness had to find its way into the worldview of the average prosperous Westerner, and that could only happen through the transformation of the culture.

What the economic and cultural Marxists had in common, though, was their antipathy to Christianity because it stood in their way. Christianity and its cultural influence must be taken down, specifically through the eradication of traditional norms and institutions. So, in 1923, a group of Marxists established the Institute for Social Research as what we call today a "think tank" associated with the University of Frankfurt in Germany.

Ironically, it was the fruits of capitalism that enabled the intellectual spade work of both the orthodox economic Marxism of Marx and the cultural Marxism of what came to be called the Frankfurt School. Karl Marx lived his entire adult life financially dependent on his intellectual partner Friedrich Engels, whose wealthy family owned large cotton-textile mills in Germany and England. It was also the fruit of hated capitalism that allowed Felix Weil to use money from his father's grain business to finance the Institute. The purpose of the Institute would be to unmask all the institutions and organs of culture that promoted and maintained the shared value systems responsible for the public support of those institutions and culture, most especially the family and religion. Paul Kengor identifies the strategy to accomplish this:

> Rather than organize the workers and the factories, the peasants and the fields and the farms, they would organize the intellectuals and the academy,

the artists and the media and the film industry. These would be the conveyor belts to deliver the fundamental transformation.[1]

The process of transformation would be helped tremendously by someone who came between Marx and the Frankfurt school who had a profound influence on the continuing secularization of Western culture, Sigmund Freud (1856-1939). Marx didn't have the discipline of psychology which developed later in the nineteenth century, nor Freudian teaching on sexuality, but the cultural Marxists did. Kengor calls what the Frankfurt school developed a kind of Freudian-Marxism, the worst of the ideas of the nineteenth century wedded with some of the worst of the twentieth.[2] Both the older and newer Marxists believed religion, i.e., Christianity, and the family had to be "abolished," as Marx put it, but the old way just didn't work. The Soviets did everything they could to snuff out both, including murdering tens of millions of their own people—religion and the family, however, just wouldn't go away. Bishop Fulton Sheen said communists failed to convince the world there is no God. Rather, they succeeded only in convincing the world there is a devil.[3]

The insights of the cultural Marxists can definitely be attributed to the devil, the diabolical genius we discussed in the last chapter. If the family is the building block of civilization, dismantling it via dysfunctional families is a shrewd strategy to accomplish that. Since the so-called sexual revolution of the 1960s, which as we'll see is the fruit of Frankfurt, it is clear how successful they have been. But like all agents of darkness, light is the great disinfectant and the revealing we are experiencing is bringing into the light the Marxist influences on our current cultural maladies.

CRITICAL THEORY AND CULTURAL REVOLUTION

Three men most influential in the founding of the Institute and its philosophical direction were not directly associated with it for various reasons, Hungarian György Lukács (1885–1971), German Karl Korsch (1886-1961), and Italian Antonio Gramsci (1891–1937). They are considered by many as the founders of "Western Marxism" which in due course became what we call cultural Marxism. In the words of Korsch what set them apart from the traditional Marxists of the time was the "critical investigation of the existing conditions" which would lead to "a transition from the present historical phase to a higher form of society." Lukács formulated a vision of Marxism as a self-conscious transformation of society rooted in the critique of *all* things in bourgeois culture. The necessity of the cultural focus as a strategy becomes clear when you read something like this:

> The proletariat only perfects itself by annihilating and transcending itself, by creating the classless society through the successful conclusion of its own class struggle. The struggle for this society, in which the dictatorship of the proletariat is merely a phase, is not just a battle waged against an external enemy, the bourgeoisie. It is equally the struggle of the proletariat against itself: against the devastating and degrading effects of the capitalist system upon its class consciousness. The proletariat will only have won the real victory when it has overcome these effects within itself.[4]

The proletariat, the working class, is being oppressed and because of that does not know they have what Marxists call a "false consciousness." They must be taught through culture, or more accurately be programmed, to accept their oppression. This brief description of Gramsci's thought shows us why these three men got along so well:

> Gramsci sought to break with Karl Marx's economic determinism and base his theory on wielding and maintaining power by the ruling class, which has commonly become known as his theory of cultural hegemony. Gramsci believed that the ruling class, the bourgeoisie, used cultural institutions to maintain power. They use ideology, rather than violence or economic force, to propagate their own values by creating the capitalist zeitgeist. Cultural hegemony is maintained by the capitalist ruling class through the institutions that make up society's superstructure. Gramscian Marxists define the superstructure as everything not directly having to do with production such as family, culture, religion, education, media, and law.[5]

He is most famous today for two ideas he developed, the first being this idea of "cultural hegemony," meaning the dominance of one group over another, often supported by legitimating norms and ideas. This dominant position of a particular set of ideas leads to them becoming commonsensical and intuitive, especially traditional religious ideas, and cultural Marxists were determined to take it all down.

The other idea for which Gramsci is well-known is the phrase, "Long march through the institutions" of culture. The phrase or something like it originated with Gramsci but was popularized as a succinct mission statement by German Communist student activist Rudi Dutschke in the 1960s. It is wise for those who are impatient with the current wokeness of American and Western culture to remember this "long march" started in the early 1920s, or one hundred years ago, so stopping and reversing that march won't happen overnight. We need to be as patient, persistent, diligent, and determined as the Marxists.

The direction of the Frankfurt school took shape primarily under the leadership of Max Horkheimer (1895–1973), a Marxist philosopher who became the Institute's director in 1930. He is most responsible for developing the academic discipline which came to be known as "critical theory." While it is apparent what critical theory is from the quotes above, it is imperative to understand that the goal of its practitioners is to tear down, to delegitimize, to stigmatize, *everything* that created Christian Western civilization over the last 2,000 years. In their minds our civilization, and all who embrace it, are the enemy and must in Marx's term be "abolished." They don't believe it will require a Soviet style tyranny, but as we've seen over the last several years in wokeness, it will be nasty. Horkheimer attracted a talented group of Marxist philosophers and social scientists—including two who would be hugely influential in establishing critical theory in American higher education, and eventually American culture—Theodor Adorno (1903–69) and Herbert Marcuse (1898–1979).

THANK YOU HITLER: HOW FRANKFURT BECAME AMERICAN

We can thank Adolf Hitler for bringing the cultural Marxism wrecking ball to America. If the Institute for Social Research had remained in Germany, cultural Marxism may have stayed isolated in Europe. However, when Hitler became Chancellor of Germany in 1933 with many in the school being Jewish, it relocated to New York City in 1935 and set up shop at Columbia University. It shouldn't surprise us that Marxists would find a welcoming home at an American university in 1935—secular academia always welcomes subversive ideas first. But even in the 1930s at the height of the Great Depression, Communism was a tough sell in America, and always would be, but in disguise as cultural Marxism, that was a different story.

After the war most of the faculty and Horkheimer went back to Germany to re-establish the school, but Marcuse decided to stay in America. Adorno returned to Germany as well but returned to America in the early 50s for a time to not lose his American citizenship. Although he returned to Germany after a time, he had a significant impact on the culture wars in America. Marcuse though was the most significant figure to come out of the Frankfurt school. He became a naturalized U.S. citizen in 1940 and served as an intelligence analyst for the precursor of the CIA from 1941 to 1944. After the war, he continued in that work for another agency, and then made his way back into academia. He taught at Columbia and Harvard universities (1951 to 1954), Brandeis University (1954–65), and the University of California, San Diego (1965–76), where after retirement he was honorary emeritus professor of philosophy until his death.

Marcuse is most famously known as the father of the "New Left" and the counterculture of the 1960s and 1970s. In addition, he was influential in the growth of political correctness and the wokeness of our time. The "Old Left" were those who embraced the old orthodox forms of Marxism, and especially that as practiced in the Soviet Union. Young Marxist radicals by contrast were disaffected with Soviet Communism and looking for new ways to bring down the capitalist West. The cultural approach of Frankfurt would come to dominate American Marxism through the pen of Marcuse. During his time in academia, he attracted young radical disciples like Angela Davis and Abbie Hoffman among many others.

Marcuse was a prolific author, but we'll briefly look at three of his most influential works that helped establish cultural Marxism in America, *Eros and Civilization, A Philosophical Inquiry into Freud* (1955), *One-Dimensional Man: Studies in the Ideology of Advanced Industrial Society* (1964), and *Repressive Tolerance* (1965). There is no need to go into detail on these other than to expose the basic ideas that eventually led to the woke world we currently endure. As with all intellectual philosophical works of the past, few normal people read these things, but the ideas percolate among intellectual elites in academia, are taught to our children, and eventually come to dominate the culture.

EROS AND CIVILIZATION

Without a doubt this book paved the way for "the sexual revolution" of the 1960s. Wilhelm Reich, also of the Frankfurt School, wrote a book in 1936 called *Sexuality in the Culture War* that had a profound influence on Marcuse, and was later published in English as *The Sexual Revolution*. It would take almost three decades before Reich's ideas would begin to permeate Western culture. As mentioned above, the Frankfurt School looked to promote a Freudian-Marxism, and *Eros and Civilization* was instrumental in accomplishing that. The basic idea is simple. Eros or libido, Freud argued, needed to be suppressed for civilization to work, while Marcuse countered that suppressing natural sexual urges enabled the exploitation inherent in capitalism of the working classes. Freud wasn't making a moral judgment because as an atheist morality wasn't his concern. He was only explaining how the dynamic of sexuality made civilization feasible. In response, Marcuse was arguing that Freud was making capitalist oppression of the proletariat inevitable.

Like other Marxists, much of what Marcuse writes is inscrutable, typically jargon-filled leftism. Carl Trueman said it perfectly:

> The New Left is a complicated movement, but it bequeathed to subsequent generations... a barbaric prose style of Gnostic opacity that cloaked its arguments in shrouds of impenetrable linguistic bombast...[6]

His influence on Western culture has little to do with how well the arguments are understood or how well he made them. Rather, the basic message the radicals of the '60s and '70s took from Marcuse was repressing sexuality is bad and liberating sexuality is good. Ergo, the sexual revolution! While most of his young acolytes at the time were basically looking for sex, Marcuse was a true believer and was only concerned about ushering in a Marxist cultural revolution. On that count we can see he was most certainly a success.

ONE-DIMENSIONAL MAN

This very influential book among the left is typical Marxist anti-capitalist pabulum. Marcuse introduces the idea of the "one dimensional man" who is subjected to a new kind of totalitarianism by consumerist and technological capitalism. In the 1960s, this critique was new to most Westerners, but since then it's become cliché. We are "blissful slaves" who willingly obey a system which keeps us distracted by being entertained and numbingly sated. To Marcuse, people under liberal Western capitalism are no freer than people under a totalitarian rule like Soviet communism. The apparatus of consumerism promotes conformity aimed at preventing resistance to the necessary need for change, i.e., revolution. This mentality is of course common on the secular left, but like the sexual revolution it has seeped into the worldview of the average Westerner.

REPRESSIVE TOLERANCE, ADORNO AND ANTI-FASCISM

While the influence of those two books in Western secular culture cannot be exaggerated, this essay is the most relevant for our historical moment. It is the inspiration for what we now call "cancel culture." Only certain accepted speech can be tolerated because actual tolerance is "repressive." Written as part of a book called *A Critique of Pure Tolerance*, Marcuse argues that "tolerance today, is in many of its most effective manifestations serving as a cause of oppression." From the perspective of a cultural Marxist, of course it is. The perverse logic of Marcuse as a cultural Marxist must be read to be believed. In this upside down, inside out world, tolerance "actually protects the already established machinery of discrimination." Free speech and the First Amendment are considered dangerous; a common trope on the left is "speech is violence." If that is true, of course it must not be tolerated, and we'll see why from Marcuse's perspective.

A deep analysis of the piece is unnecessary, but part of his argument will serve to introduce us to one other influential member of the Frankfurt School mentioned above, Theodor Adorno. What Adorno did in 1950 allowed Marcuse to develop "the Nazi argument." It was a diabolically genius move paying cultural dividends to this day. First Marcuse lays his cards on the table:

> Liberating tolerance... would mean intolerance against movements from the Right, and toleration of movements from the left.

How convenient, but we'll see why he says this when we get to Adorno. Then he gives us the punch line:

> In past and different circumstances, the speeches of the Fascist and Nazi leaders were the immediate prologue to the massacre. The distance between the propaganda and the action, between the organization and its release on the people had become too short. But the spreading of the word could have been stopped before it was too late: if democratic tolerance had been withdrawn when the future leaders started their campaign, mankind would have had a chance of avoiding Auschwitz and a World War.[7]

It's a short trip from this to "speech is violence," and by definition it can *only* be speech from the right. This led to a common phrase the New Left used in their protests against the Vietnam War in the 1960s, "No free speech for Fascists." Thus, what we know as cancel culture is a necessity to keep the right from doing what Fascists and Nazi's always do. Not cancelling people on the right and their speech would be a dereliction of duty, the First Amendment be damned. Of course, all the political violence is on the left, but that is justified violence because it's used against the Fascist right. A group using violence today can be called Antifa, for anti-fascists, with a straight face. You can't make this stuff up!

Adorno was the one who made this connection in his 1950 book *The Authoritarian Personality*. Dinesh D'Souza in his book *The Big Lie: Exposing the Nazi Roots of the American*

Left has a section titled, "The Deceitful Origin of 'Anti-Fascism.'" He writes that after World War II:

> Nazism became the very measure of evil. So Marcuse and Adorno knew that anything associated with Nazism or fascism would automatically be tainted. They set about putting this obvious fact to political use on behalf of the political Left.[8]

Fascism in this distortion of reality would now be associated with capitalism and moral traditionalism, which as we've seen must be "abolished."

D'Souza argues persuasively that Marxism and fascism are ideologies of the left, but because of Adorno they came to be associated with two different ends of the ideological and political spectrum. In his book Adorno introduced the F-Scale, in D'Souza's words:

> The basic argument was that fascism is a form of authoritarianism and that the worst manifestation of authoritarianism is self-imposed repression. Fascism develops early and we can locate it in young people's attachments to religious superstition and conventual middle-class values about family, sex, and society.[9]

So, a la Marx, religion and the family must be "abolished." The book and ideas were swallowed hook, line, and sinker by an already liberal academia and media, becoming the accepted perspective that fascism was a phenomenon of the right. It's a complete lie, but that's what Marxists do.

WOKENESS TAKES OVER AMERICAN CULTURE

In a well-known exchange in *The Sun Also Rises*, Ernest Hemingway wrote: "How did you go bankrupt?" Bill asked. "Two ways," Mike said. "Gradually, then suddenly."[10]

Gradually and suddenly perfectly describes the apparent suddenness of woke ideology completely taking over American culture the last handful of years. Like most people I was surprised but I shouldn't have been. Not only had the Frankfurt School and cultural Marxism come to America in the 1930s, but as it took root with the leftist radicals in the '60s and '70s, those people went into academia and brought their cultural Marxism with them. From there many went into education and programmed a generation of children who are now adults into the woke Marxist worldview. This process has been going on for decades and it was only a matter of time before we experienced the cultural and governing effects we have now.

The modern-day cultural Marxists, the wokesters, have been programmed, or more accurately brainwashed, into Marx's dialectical worldview of critique and crisis—or conflict theory. In a nutshell, according to Marx, those with wealth and power try to hold on to it by any means possible, mainly by suppressing the poor and powerless. A basic premise of conflict theory is that individuals and groups within society will always work to maximize their own wealth and power. It's an ugly view of reality which creates ugly people. All relationships are power struggles.

> Vladimir Lenin argued that the oppressed cannot of their own accord sufficiently understand the depths of their oppression and, therefore, need an intellectual

class continually reminding them to be angry and feel hated.[11]

Leftists push this emotional narrative of outrage which becomes axiomatic and unchallengeable. Those who do must be silenced.

Wealth and economic power are no longer part of the oppression equation because the left, the cultural Marxists, are incredibly wealthy and have all the cultural and political power. Therefore the "poor and powerless" of Marx are transferred to the culturally oppressed which has nothing to do with economics. There are many in the parade of victims we're familiar with, including "people of color" which makes white people, especially males, the oppressors. Religious minorities are oppressed as well, which makes Christians (in the West) the oppressors. The most popular of the oppressed are the sexual minorities like lesbians, homosexuals, transgendered, etc. which makes heterosexuals the oppressors. There is even something comically evil called intersectionality which creates a hierarchy of oppression. At the top of the oppression scale would be white heterosexual Christian males, the worst of the worst, especially those married with families. Next in line would be heterosexual women again married with families. Single women regardless of their sexuality are always lower on the scale (meaning they are more easily oppressed) than married women. Any person of color regardless of sexual preference, marital status, or religious conviction is always lower on the scale, and so on. In addition, in the woke narrative any form of inequality is equivalent to oppression, and the full oppression matrix is the means to the end of total societal transformation into a Marxist Utopia, or whatever. In practice there is no such thing, so perpetual revolution via perpetual criticism is the result—misery forever.

This would be amusing if it were not taken so seriously by the entirety of Western cultural and political elites. In fact, Elon Musk, now of unmasking Twitter fame, said in one of his red pill Tweets, "The woke mind virus is either defeated or nothing else matters." He realized this not just because of "cancel culture" and how the social media giants use their power to silence anyone who strays from the government-woke culture narrative, but because it has infected every area of society. It's even difficult to watch sports without encountering wokeness. The kids who've become adults and been indoctrinated into wokeness now not only run America's largest corporations, but they also populate all the human resources and legal departments to make sure corporate leaders toe the line. Which brings us to *Woke, Inc.* the title of a book by Vivek Ramaswamy. This bacillus of wokeness has taken over the highest of high finance and corporate governance and Ramaswamy lays out in detail how that's been done.

Ramaswamy argues that "wokeness has made American capitalism in its own image," as he calls it, "the woke-industrial complex." The phrase is a take-off from President Eisenhower's farewell address in January 1961, but Eisenhower at the height of the Cold War was warning of a "Military-Industrial Complex." I will quote Eisenhower to make Ramaswamy's point:

> In the councils of government, we must guard against the acquisition of unwarranted influence, whether sought or unsought, by the military-industrial complex. The potential for the disastrous rise of misplaced power exists and will persist. We must never

let the weight of this combination endanger our liberties or democratic processes. We should take nothing for granted. Only an alert and knowledgeable citizenry can compel the proper meshing of the huge industrial and military machinery of defense with our peaceful methods and goals, so that security and liberty may prosper together.

Eisenhower was correct and the last 50-plus years has made that readily apparent. He could never imagine a cultural Cold War even more pernicious and dangerous to "our liberties or democratic processes" using a woke-industrial complex. Ramaswamy details how this works in his book, and make no mistake, this is the way big business is run today in America. It's impossible to deny that assertion looking at the last few years:

Large banks like Goldman Sachs are particularly adept at playing the woke capitalist game. But in reality, by 2020 it was the prevailing business model in corporate America. Stakeholder capitalism—the trendy idea that companies should serve not just their shareholders but also other interests and society at large—is no longer simply on the rise. It has been crowned as the governing philosophy for big business in America.[12]

He argues that corporations are in fact really feigning wokeness for favorable government treatment, this being another form of corporate welfare.

For most of the left's existence, big business and corporations were the bad guys. If capitalism was bad, then the biggest benefactors of capitalism were the worst of the bad. The woke revolution allowed big business to virtue signal to the woke cabal that they are now the good guys. Ramaswamy writes:

> Corporations were no longer the oppressors. Instead, corporate power—if wielded in the right way—could actually empower the new disempowered classes who suffered not at the hands of evil corporations but instead at the hands of straight white men, the real culprits of oppression.[13]

Of course, the right way is the woke way, so companies like Disney are now in the business of pushing transgender ideology to children through their entertainment. Examples need not detain us because they are legion and we're all too familiar with them. The reason this is happening is found in classrooms all over America, and to that we'll turn next.

CHAPTER 8

HOW MARXISM INFILTRATED EDUCATION AND THE CLASSICAL ANSWER

As we've seen, the two primary enemies of Marxism in whatever forms it takes are Christianity and the family, and both must be abolished. Therefore it follows, the primary bulwarks against tyrannical Marxism and for liberty are Christianity and the family.

THE PRIMACY OF THE FAMILY IN EDUCATION

Western civilization and all its blessings will be restored, and Marxist wokism defeated, only to the degree Christianity and the family flourish. Our current societal collapse is what happens when these civilizational bulwarks wither.

I came across some quotes about the family from President Theodore Roosevelt that in our day would be considered "controversial," but in the early twentieth century were common:

> It is in the life of the family upon which in the last analysis the whole welfare of the Nation rests... The nation is nothing but the aggregate of the families

within its borders—Everything in the American civilization and nation rests upon the home—The family relation is the most fundamental, the most important of all relations.[1]

His traditional conception of the family including the roles of men and women as husbands and wives would be positively shocking to our secular cultural elites, woke or not. R.J. Rushdoony states what Roosevelt observed as axiomatic for Christian Western civilization:

> The family is, sociologically and religiously, the basic institution, man's first and truest government, school, state, and church. Man's basic emotional and psychic needs are met in terms of the family.[2]

This was an inarguable statement of fact until the twentieth century and the rise of secularism. With that rise the state slowly began to usurp the prerogatives of the family in education. J. Gresham Machen writing in 1925 argued it had already happened:

> The most important Christian educational institution is not the pulpit or the school, as important as these institutions are; it is the Christian family. And that institution has to a very large extent ceased to do its work... The lamentable fact is that the Christian home, as an educational institution, has largely ceased to function.[3]

The reason I start this chapter focused on the centrality of the family is not only because of the fundamental antagonism between Marxism and the family, but because wherever we come down on the nature of education in America on which Christians will disagree, we must all agree with Machen that the education of children is primarily the responsibility of the family.

Being to some degree ignorant of these matters when our children were school age, we sent them to the local public schools. Never for a moment, though, did I think it was the school's responsibility to educate my children. Yes, the schools would teach them the "three Rs," while my wife and I would teach them a Christian worldview. Interrogating them about what they were learning at school, and exploring the hidden assumptions, was a common practice in our home. It wasn't until 2010 when our daughter went off to Hillsdale College that I began to hear about this thing called Classical Education. It shocks me given my love of the liberal arts and wide reading that I don't remember ever hearing of it before then; now I'm a classical education evangelist!

In 2012, my wife worked at the elementary school our youngest son attended and was growing increasingly dismayed with what she was witnessing in public education. She insisted that he not attend our local public middle school; unfortunately, a private school was a pipe dream as far as I was concerned. There was no way we could afford it financially, and our other kids survived the public schools, faith intact, and so would he. It's pathetic when surviving is the criteria by which I judged an education for our children, but we had no choice, I thought. Thankfully, my mother-in-law decided she would cover the tuition, and our son entered Covenant Classical School in Naperville, Illinois for the fifth grade. To say I was blown away by the education we encountered at this Christian classical school would be a massive understatement. Our daughter in the meantime had decided to minor in classical education, and upon graduation worked for eight years at a charter classical school, and currently works for Hillsdale's Barney Charter Initiative (more on that later).

Even with our son at a Christian classical school, in my mind the ideal along with home schooling, his education was still our responsibility.

GOVERNMENT AND EDUCATION NEED TO GET A DIVORCE

America's founders believed deeply in the importance of education, and to that end the Continental Congress in July 1787 passed The Northwest Ordinance in which they stated:

> Religion, morality, and knowledge, being necessary to good government and the happiness of mankind, schools and the means of education shall forever be encouraged.

Religion, to the Founders, meant Christianity, and its morality and knowledge was necessary to good government and a happy populace. In other words, civilization depended on education specifically informed by religion, i.e., Christianity. It didn't follow, though, that encouragement meant government control of education given the Founders' deep suspicion of human nature and government power. Yet, over time "public" education came to mean government education subsidized by taxpayers controlled by the government. In this sense, public education is an oxymoron. Machen put this presciently in 1934:

> Every lover of human freedom ought to oppose with all his might the giving of federal aid to the schools of

this country; for federal aid in the long run inevitably means federal control, and federal control means control by a centralized and irresponsible bureaucracy, and control by such a bureaucracy means the death of everything that might make this country great.[4]

Who can argue with this after 90 years of hindsight? Rushdoony further makes our point, writing in 1961:

> The public school is now unmistakably a state school, and its concept of education is inevitably statist. This is apparent in various ways. First of all, education has ceased to be a responsibility of the home and has become a responsibility of the state... the state still claims sole right to determine the nature, extent, and time of education. Thus, a basic family right has been destroyed and the state's control over the child asserted.[5]

It cannot be both state and family, only either/or. And this is not just an argument for liberty over or against government tyranny, but a fundamentally religious question. I argued in the chapter on secularism that neutrality is a myth, and American public schools are the establishment of a secular religion in the guise of religious neutrality. Joe Boot explains:

> We can clearly see . . . that neither the *structure within* which we educate, nor the *purpose for* which we educate, nor the *content by* which we educate, can be neutral.[6]

Doug Wilson states why this an indisputable fact:

> Education is fundamentally religious. Consequently, there is no question about whether a morality will be imposed in that education, but rather which morality will be imposed. Christians and assorted tradition- alists who want a secular school system to install anything other than secular ethics are wanting some- thing that has never happened and can never happen.[7]

He further asserts that public or "common schools were going to be the means by which the entire progressive agenda was ushered in."[8] Progressive in the twenty-first century is nothing like the early progressives imagined, but in hindsight it's easy to see how secular progressive education paved the way for a takeover of education by cultural Marxists.

Does this mean that what we know as public education needs to be "abolished," to borrow from Marx? Yes! School choice may be a good stopgap measure to take away some of the monopoly power of the government, but it is only tem- porary. It follows from the biblical imperative of the familial responsibility of the educating of children, that it must be completely private and divorced from government at any level. Government money always brings with it govern- ment influence. Education is a worldview enterprise, and in America parents should be free to decide in what worldview they want their children educated.

What that looks like and how we get there I don't know. I only know this should be the objective of any Christian who understands the incompatibility of Christianity with any other worldview in the educating of children. In the mean- time, as we work toward this, I believe that charter classical

schools are a critical means to challenging the secular progressive monopoly on education.

THE RISE OF PROGRESSIVE EDUCATION IN AMERICA

Conservatives have been complaining about public education for a very long time. In fact, a popular book called *Why
Johnny Can't Read—And What You Can Do About It* came out
in 1955. Some people think the 1950s was the golden age of
conservatism. It wasn't. That decade continued the consequences of secular progressivism in American culture, even
if the effects were masked by leftover conservative Christian
cultural influence. Education was a fundamental part of the
progressive vision of transforming America into a "modern"
democracy based on "scientific" principles among other
things, and progressives paved the way for what has become
the Marxification of education.

Progressive education goes back well before there
was a progressive movement in America to the influence of Horace Mann (1796-1859), considered the father
of American public schools. Like most nineteenth century reformers, Mann was a "conservative progressive"
in that he pushed progressive reforms for conservative
ends. Once Christian culture was no longer dominant in
the twentieth century conservative ends went out the window. As a reformer, he convinced Americans they should
pay for public, or "common," schools, and established
the Massachusetts State Board of Education. According to
Britannica, Mann "believed that, in a democratic society, education should be free and universal, nonsectarian, democratic in method, and reliant on well-trained
professional teachers." We can see immediately from a
Christian perspective this is a non-starter, yet not only did

it start, but in due course this perspective took over education in America.

To reiterate, there can be no such thing as a "nonsectarian" education because education is fundamentally religious and always inculcates a worldview in the children being educated. Also, there is no such thing as free education. In practice, free always means someone else pays. There is no constitutional right in America to insist that other Americans pay for my children's education, or that I pay for theirs. Yet by the twentieth century this became an unquestioned dogma, and if challenged, charges from the left erupted like a volcano, hot and fast. Nonsectarian eventually became in practice the progressive secular religion.

Doug Wilson tells how these reformers were uniformly hostile to orthodox Christianity. Many were Unitarians, the number one Christian heresy of the day. As he points out, the local government schools were mostly run by Christians who had no idea the true intent of the reformers above them. If the communities were Evangelical, so were the schools, but the secular progressive die was cast. He writes of one nineteenth century Cassandra, R.L. Dabney (1820-1898), whose prophecies of the inevitable consequences proved true. Dabney wrote:

> We have seen that their [the schools'] complete secularization is logically inevitable. Christians must prepare themselves then, for the following results: All prayer, catechisms, and Bibles will ultimately be driven out of the schools.[9]

At the behest of radical atheist Madalyn Murray O'Hair, the Supreme Court in 1962 basically outlawed prayer in public schools—nonsectarian indeed.

Arguably the Olympic champion of progressive education was John Dewey (1859-1952) who was passionate about "democracy," and education as the way to achieve it. As in everything else in the history of ideas and culture, Dewey's philosophy was the result of a long chain of intellectual and cultural events going back a very long time. The Enlightenment is a favorite conservative Christian whipping boy, and rightly so, but the Enlightenment came from somewhere. The point is that cultural transformation starts with education, and the torrent of secular, progressive ideas like a rushing river had momentum by the late nineteenth century that would not be stopped. The torrent, however, has hit a wall because of cultural Marxism and the rebound is exposing lies and revealing truth to millions of Americans. Before we see what that looks like, a little about the influential John Dewey is in order.

The basic outline of Dewey's influence is found in the word progressive itself; it had to be different than whatever came before, and unfortunately it was. Prior to the progressive era, education in America was basically classical. Progressives believed "classical" was against "progress," so it had to go. Here is a smattering of Dewey's ideas:

- Education should promote the practical over the abstract.
- Experience was the great teacher, and the scientific method the primary source of knowledge.
- The idea of "public" should replace the "individual."
- Traditional religion, i.e., Christianity, is an obstacle to true education and progress.
- Human nature is not fixed but can be changed via education.

- Traditional classrooms stifle a child's curiosity, creativity, and excitement for learning.
- Discipline or correction is not a teacher's duty, but rather to understand and follow a student's interest and impulses.
- The utility of ideas is what makes them important.
- Education is not primarily about academics or morality, but societal change.
- Goals and standards are harmful to a child's motivation.
- Pedagogy must be a discipline apart from subject matter and methodology takes precedence over content.

Henry T. Edmondson summarizes Dewey's influence well:

> Thanks in no small part to Dewey, much of what characterizes contemporary education is a revolt against various expressions of authority: a revolt against a canon of learning, a revolt against tradition, a revolt against religious values, a revolt against moral standards, a revolt against logic—even a revolt against grammar and spelling.[10]

And a mighty successful revolt it has been! But now there is a counter revolt happening as the poverty of progressive education and its Marxist progeny becomes impossible to ignore.

Part of the poverty is covered in the last bullet point. Machen highlights what I think is the most important deception of progressive education. Writing in 1932, it was already axiomatic in education circles:

> It never seems to occur to many modern teachers that the primary business of the teacher is to study the

subject that he is going to teach. Instead... he studies "education"; a knowledge of the methodology of
teaching takes the place of a knowledge of the particular branch of literature, history, or science to which
a man has devoted his life.[11]

The pedagogy of methodology over content was a perfect breeding ground for what came next, the Marxification
of Education.

HOW CULTURAL MARXISM TOOK OVER EDUCATION

If we better understood the cultural Marxists' influence
in education the apparent suddenness of the wokification
of American culture would not have surprised us. Nearly
every day I encounter people incredulous that such things as
Drag Queen Story Hour and transgenderism, or Critical Race
Theory, or any number of other perversions are being taught
and promoted in our public and private schools. This apparent success, as counter intuitive as it may seem, came from
the failure of traditional economic Marxism. By the 1970s,
the New Left had precipitated a very real cultural revolution,
but when Reagan was elected the Marxists were distraught.
How could this happen! What about "the revolution"? Now,
they thought, another fascist is running America. James
Lindsey in his book, *The Marxification of Education*, tells us
the story of how this happened.[12]

This seeming failure led them to realize that in "the
long march through the institutions" the most important
institution, by far, was education. Without capturing education, the Marxists had no way to overcome what they called
the "the problem of reproduction." Simply put, a culture
reproduces itself through education. All the enemies of the

revolution—family, religion, traditional values, capitalism—all of it was continuing to be reproduced unless they did something about it. Then Brazilian educator and philosopher, Paulo Freire (1921-1997), entered the picture. So important is Freire in Lindsay's opinion that he's in the subtitle of his book. It's stunning to me someone so influential in contributing to the destruction of Christian Western civilization is almost completely unknown among conservatives.

Distressed by the lack of a communist revolution, Freire came to the realization that the purpose of education isn't learning per se, but "raising Marxist political consciousness for the purpose of creating a cultural revolution."[13] Now, according to Lindsay, kids go to "Paulo Freire schools," and what happens there may appear to be education but is in fact political brainwashing. This happened strategically. The Marxist New Left radicals of the 60s and 70s were encouraged to go into education to make what Lindsay calls "the theft of education":

> The mechanism... was straightforward and generational: capture and transform the colleges of education; mold a generation of teachers; program every generation of students thereafter. Colleges of education were captured almost entirely to the Freirean approach by no later than 1995, and the intervening quarter century has seen enough turnover of the teachers to have fundamentally remade our schools and thus education itself.[14]

In fact, this has been so successful that "Freire is recognized as the third most-cited scholarly author in all of the humanities and social sciences by authoritative metrics."[15] That is scary.

If you read the last two chapters, none of this will be news to you. The goal of education is not learning things but teaching students how to view the world from the "standpoint of the oppressed." Critical pedagogy, or criticizing all perpetuating oppressive power structures, is done by denouncing the "dehumanizing conditions" of the world. Freire introduced a word that explains the process of making this happen: "conscientization."[16] What it does, very effectively, is create Marxists of little children who become Marxist teenagers and eventually Marxist adults who run most all the important institutions of American culture. A generation of students who have been "conscientized" now run major corporations, professional sports teams, legacy media and most Big Tech, entertainment, much of law and government, and so on. They infect the HR and legal departments, so even those who are not woke must kowtow to the reigning orthodoxy or risk losing their living.

The beauty of the Marxist conflict model from their perspective is that it can apply to any area of knowledge, literally. Nothing in society is free from the withering criticism because it all perpetuates oppression and stands in the way of revolutionary consciousness. Regardless of the topic, "that domain of thought unjustly recognizes certain privileged knowledges, knowers, and ways of knowing while excluding and marginalizing others to its own benefit."[17] According to Lindsay, one of the main ways to instill the correct, i.e., Marxist, way of knowing is through a "generative" process. The most successful and pernicious way this is done is through something called Social-Emotional Learning. It sounds harmless enough and made to appear that way. I did a quick search and found this right at the top:

> Social-emotional learning (SEL) is the process of developing the self-awareness, self-control, and interpersonal skills that are vital for school, work, and life success.[18]

More accurately, SEL is Marxist indoctrination to program our children to become woke robots for the revolution. I don't have room to get into details of how this works, but one detail Lindsay covers is Comprehensive Sexuality Education. This uses "a generative (Freirean) pedagogical approach" to encourage children to learn to:

> live "queerly" which is defined as a (Marxist-style) opposition to any and all norms or conceptions of normalcy, especially with regard to sex, gender, and sexuality.[19]

So schools promoting Drag Queen Story hour should not surprise us, nor that some parents actually welcome it. They've become good little Marxist robots because that's how they were educated (Lindsay argues brainwashed).

THE BACKLASH AND REASON FOR OPTIMISM

One reason I'm excited about the prospect for the future of America, and the West in general, is that Marxists are finally being exposed for what they are. And no matter how much push-back they get, like all good progressives they double down which in turn only wakes up more people to the irrational evil of their worldview. An increasing number of Americans, and people throughout the Western world, are realizing we can't coexist with these people; they *must* be defeated. Thankfully, the true believers, those who would prefer to die on the woke battlefield than ever give up, are a tiny minority of the population. The only way woke wins is through dishonesty, lies, stolen elections, and the weaponization of the law against any who dare question the woke status quo. These tactics only work so long—then the Berlin Wall falls.

There are innumerable examples of people who have seen the light, and I've been introduced to many of them on Steve Bannon's *War Room*. The awakening coming from the over-reach of the Commies, as I affectionately call them, is truly remarkable and inspiring. Almost every day I'm being introduced to new people who have had it and are fed up. In the words of longtime news anchor Howard Beale in the 1975 film classic *Network*, "I'm mad as hell and I'm not going to take it anymore!" Unlike the movie, however, the current frustration breeding this growing backlash is not a parable for the futility of our anger. In the coming chapters I will make the case why real, substantive, and lasting change is coming, and why in the title and words of a famous song of the same era from The Who: "We Won't Get Fooled Again!"

One inspiring example of this backlash is a group called Moms for Liberty, founded by two moms from Florida who were former school board members and had experienced enough of the insanity. They decided to build an organization that would stand up for parental rights at all levels of government. They and many other fed-up parents were instrumental in the 2021 Virginia gubernatorial election of Glenn Younkin over the woke former governor of the state. Before 2020 and before wokeness exploded on the scene few concerned themselves with school board races. Now, scrutiny by parents and other organizations is part of the job description. More parents than ever are realizing their children's education is ultimately their responsibility, and that's something we can build on as we fight the government domination of our schools.

WHY CLASSICAL EDUCATION IS THE ANSWER

As mentioned previously, education in America prior to the progressive takeover was for the most part classical. In case you're like me prior to 2010 when I was, sadly, completely ignorant on the subject, I want to briefly explain what classical education is and why it is the answer. Thankfully, I have access to a classical education professional who can make the case much better than I can; my daughter, Gabrielle Lewis, is going to do that for me:

Classical education is a particular philosophy of education, which, prior to the onset of progressive education in the late 1800's, was known simply as "education." All educated persons were once classically, or synonymously, "liberally" educated. From the ancient Greeks and Romans and later given form by academics in the Middle Ages, we received the "liberal arts and sciences." The liberal arts were thought to free the mind from the bondage of ignorance. The focus of K–12 classical education includes three of the liberal arts, grammar, logic, and rhetoric, known as the *trivium*, or "the three-fold path." These three are central disciplines because they are the foundation of how one learns—the tools used to come to knowledge of the self, of nature, and of the cosmos. Grammar, logic, and rhetoric train the mind in the art of learning. Classically speaking, the goal of education is to foster intellectual and moral virtue, and to train the mind to seek truth so that students might think and learn for themselves. Classical education promotes inquiry which allows students to discover for themselves what is good, true, and beautiful.

Much of the educational model in classical schools is taken from Dorothy Sayers' essay presented at Oxford in 1947, "The Lost Tools of Learning." She was the first to link the trivium to the stages of development of a grade-school-aged child, and how a child learns as he or she matures. In the grammar stage (K-5), children are like parrots; they eagerly memorize things by heart and recite them ad nauseum. Their little minds are like proverbial sponges, soaking up anything and everything they can learn and then repeating it over and over. At this stage students gain basic facts to build a foundation of knowledge, allowing them to proceed into the next stage of learning, the dialectic (or logic stage). Logic-aged students, roughly 6th-8th graders, have a knack for arguing and for asking, "How do I know this is true, good, or right?" Capitalizing on this, classical schools train their pupils in the art of logic, or argumentation. Learning the tools of reasoning, students organize what they gleaned on a basic level in grammar school and learn to evaluate and analyze it properly. It isn't until the rhetoric stage (9th-12th grade) that students formulate fallacy-free opinions of all they have received and learn to express these opinions eloquently in both speech and writing. At this stage students digest all they have learned and make the knowledge their own by grappling with it and defending it to others. This process—understanding, evaluating, and then expressing an opinion of those facts—is the foundation of learning anything well.

The *trivium* are the "tools of learning," and it is by these tools that students crack the challenging code of discovering how to learn throughout life. In addition to developing a love of learning in children, they will have formed a good and virtuous character. Learning something well is hard and takes immense discipline and perseverance; but as Aristotle proclaimed, although the roots of education are bitter, the fruit it yields is sweet.

Every time Gabrielle or my son-in-law, also a classical educator, talk about classical education, I get excited all over again.

Because of the worldview and fundamentally religious nature of education, the ideal school environment for Christians and their children is the Christian Classical School. Doug Wilson makes the argument in *A Case for Christian Classical Education*, and I completely agree with him. One of the reasons in addition to not wanting a foreign worldview inculcated into our children, is that Christian classical education done right "is nothing less than Christian civilization."[20] As re-forming Western Christian civilization is one of the goals of this book, I certainly agree with that too. Unfortunately, in the current historical moment that is an option for only a limited number of Christian parents. In addition, there are 50 million children going to public schools every day, and they are being indoctrinated in cultural Marxism. Charter classical schools are a way to save children from that fate and contribute to saving America.

Not only that, but a child who attends and graduates from a charter classical school will not be as susceptible to the lies of woke culture. They will also appreciate the role of Christianity in shaping Western civilization, and likely become allies in its re-birth. I would also argue that a student graduating from a charter classical school will have a worldview more in common with Christianity, and possibly be more open to Christianity itself. Just learning in an environment that teaches the objective nature of reality and truth is a significant advance from the other public alternatives.

I will end this with the "Key Characteristics of Hillsdale Classical Schools" from their website, and you compare this to any other public school in America, and the case makes itself:

1. A curriculum that is content-rich, balanced, and strong across the four disciplines of math, science, literature, and history

2. Instruction in the Western tradition through history, literature, philosophy, and the fine arts

3. Study of the American literary, moral, philosophical, political, and historical traditions

4. Explicit instruction in phonics and grammar

5. The study of Latin as a requirement for all students

6. An approach to instruction that acknowledges objective standards of correctness, logic, beauty, weightiness, and truth

7. A well-educated and articulate faculty who use traditional, teacher-led methods of instruction

8. A commitment to use technology effectively without diminishing the faculty leadership that is crucial to academic achievement

9. A plan to serve Grades K through 12 (even if the school must open with fewer grades) so as to provide continuity and a recurrent examination of subjects throughout a student's career

10. A school culture of moral virtue, decorum, respect, discipline, and studiousness among both students and faculty

A day or so after I sent my daughter this chapter so she could write her section on classical education, we got a magazine in the mail addressed to her because she lived with us before she got married and we still get it. It's called *The Classical Teacher* from Memoria Press, a publishing company that produces classical Christian education materials for home and private schools. I noticed the tag line on its cover: Saving Western civilization one student at time. That says it all.

CHAPTER 9
PROGRESSIVISM, PROGRESS AND GLOBALIST TYRANNY

The history of progressivism in America is a fascinating study helping us understand the great reveal we are living through. The seeds of this movement started germinating in various reform movements with the most noble of motives in the nineteenth century, sprouted into full maturity with a remarkable hubris in the twentieth, and turned into the woke tyrannical movement it is today. As soon as the sapling of progressivism broke ground its destruction was inevitable. It should be clear from the last several chapters how this happened, and what its antecedents were. I could have easily placed this chapter after my treatment of secularism because secularism was the driver of progressivism, and cultural Marxism was just the latest hitchhiker on the secular gravy train easily highjacked for its woke purposes. It was important, however, to explain the birth of cultural Marxism and how progressivism gave up without a fight, both movements being primarily secular.

It is also instructive to note that until only recently progressives preferred to be called liberals because who wants to be illiberal. It's also easier to paint the conservative opposition as just that. The opposite of progressive is of course regressive, and nobody wants to be that either, but progressive is a more apt description for a movement that intends to be going somewhere forward, away from the past, while the term liberalism doesn't convey movement of any kind—that just won't do. And as I argued in the first two chapters, the great reveal that's happened since Trump came down the escalator, while not exactly separating the sheep from the goats, has definitely separated the liberals who are truly liberal, from progressives who most certainly are not.

PROGRESS AND THE SPIRIT OF NINETEENTH CENTURY AMERICA

It's striking to look back on this side of the unimaginable suffering and misery of the twentieth century to realize just how much progress obsessed post-Civil War America. George Marsden observes that "in a nation born during the Enlightenment, the reverence for science as the way to understand all aspects of reality was nearly unbounded."[1] This reverence grew out of the heady Enlightenment assumption that science and reason could solve all mankind's problems eventually. The stunning advances in technology seemed to justify the hubris. A good indicator of this is utility patent applications, which cover the most common forms of inventions. In 1850 there were 2,193, and by 1900 that had grown to 36,673. That's more than sixteen times the number annually, and it went up from there. The railroad and the telegraph changed transportation and communications in ways previously unthinkable, and electricity transformed night into day. On May 1, 1893, at the Chicago World's Fair, President Grover Cleveland pushed a button, and 100,000 incandescent lamps illuminated the White City (so named because almost all the buildings were painted white). This was such a dazzling achievement that the world literally beat a path to the door of what had then come to be known as the "Second City" only to New York.

All these changes were part of the industrial revolution after the Civil War, transforming the largely agrarian society of America's founding into a worldwide economic powerhouse. Along with change came problems. Industrialization and growing populations of immigrants flocking to cities along the East coast created deplorable conditions for a significant number of people. Christians thought Christianity provided an answer in what came to be known as the Social Gospel, and a significant change in American Christianity was on the horizon.

Many nineteenth century reformers, like the abolitionists, were Unitarians having rejected what they considered the illogical concept of the Trinity; their hearts were in the right place, but their theology wasn't. German biblical criticism and its rejection of the Bible as reliable history and God's authoritative verbal revelation had a profound effect on Christianity in the growing secular age. The spreading rejection of orthodox historic Christianity in the mainline denominations, along with the suffering brought on by the industrial revolution, produced the response of the Social Gospel. Addressing woeful material conditions took priority over the spiritual condition of someone's soul. After all, wasn't concern for the poor and suffering a hallmark of Jesus' and the Apostles' ministry? Indeed it was, but he also said, "For what will it profit a man if he gains the whole world and forfeits his soul? Or what shall a man give in return for his soul?" (Matt. 16:26).

This struggle for the soul of Christianity (pun intended) was played out in the late nineteenth and early twentieth centuries and came to be called the fundamentalist-modernist controversies. From the late 1870s to Word War I, the leadership of mainline Protestant denominations slowly but surely gave up any pretense of believing the Bible was a supernatural document. They accepted the Enlightenment assumptions of empiricism and rationalism, including the inevitable conclusion of German biblical critics' attacks on its veracity. These were the liberals, and conservatives who stood against them came to be called fundamentalists from a series of twelve short books, *The Fundamentals*, written from 1910 to 1915. Even though he was a conservative, William Jennings Bryan echoed what almost all Christians believed prior to World War I:

> Christian civilization is the greatest that the world has ever known because it rests on a conception of life that makes life one unending progress toward higher things, with no limit to human advancement or development.[2]

As George Marsden adds, "evangelicals generally regarded almost any sort of progress as evidence of the advance of the kingdom."[3]

In the 1890s the work of a group of journalists called muckrakers (a term of derision painted on them by Teddy Roosevelt) put motivation into the social gospel movement. They exposed the widespread suffering in America's cities that could not be ignored and prompted the coalescing of the various reform movements into a progressive movement. Most agree the "progressive era" officially started 1901 with the unexpected presidency of Theodore Roosevelt after the assassination of President McKinley. It would be a mistake, however, to think of Roosevelt in any way like what progressives became as the century wore on, but he was certainly part of a mission to change the way American government interacted with society.

In the mind of progressives, his presidency brought with it a growing conviction that government was instrumental in creating the just society of America's founding promise. Without government intervention these problems would remain insoluble; without the power of the state anarchy and suffering would reign. Liberal Christians agreed. Progressives' contention would become increasingly clear: the government of America's founding, built for an agrarian society of primarily farmers and ranchers with a relatively small homogeneous population, was no match for a modern industrial society. Woodrow Wilson saw the U.S. Constitution as an antiquated document for another time and not up to the new realities of modern government. From Wilson would flow into the progressive bloodstream the idea of a "living constitution," which is of course no constitution at all. Holding the firm conviction that with science and technology no problem seemed too big to overcome, progressives were determined to apply this mindset to government. Something called "scientific" management or planning by "experts" would become the rallying cry of the new century.

Conservatives are fond of saying ideas have consequences, from the title of Ricard Weaver's influential 1948 book. Of course they do, but technology and scientific advancement do as well. The cultural shifts of the nineteenth century driven by the ideas of the Enlightenment were enhanced by the massive technological achievements changing the way Americans lived and viewed the world. American culture of the late nineteenth century was a very different place than in the late eighteenth century. This transformation drove the progressive freight train into the twentieth century to begin the fundamental transformation of America Barack Obama promised a hundred years later—there was a significant amount of transformation before he came on the stage. The very idea of progress was itself transformed.

THE BASTARDIZATION OF "PROGRESS"

These cultural consequences had profound worldview implications bound up in a simple word now loaded with metaphysical meaning. Science and technology were not only seen as the solutions to the abundant problems confronting the modern world, but the conviction grew that man himself could solve them all in the pursuit of progress, the means to our material salvation. Most historians agree that science grew out of the Christian worldview, and its foundations built by Christians such as Kepler, Boyle, Faraday, and Newton. The growing secularism of the Enlightenment, though, caused people to dissociate science from its Christian roots in humble discovery of God's ridiculously complex created world. Instead, it became the fuel for man's hubris trying to build a modern tower of Babel. Science transformed into Scientism. J.P. Moreland defines scientism as,

> roughly the view that the hard sciences—like chemistry, biology, physics, astronomy—provide the only genuine knowledge of reality. At the very least, this scientific knowledge is vastly superior to what we can know from any other discipline.[4]

It's impossible to tell exactly when the concept of progress changed, considering cultural currents aren't given to exactness, but as early as 1905 the great English journalist G.K. Chesterton understood that the modern notion of progress had distorted the word beyond measure:

> Every one of the popular modern phrases and ideals is a dodge in order to shirk the problem of what is good. We are fond of talking about "liberty"; that, as we talk of it, is a dodge to avoid discussing what is good. We are fond of talking about "progress"; that is a dodge to avoid discussing what is good. We are fond of talking about "education"; that is a dodge to avoid discussing what is good. The modern man says, "Let us leave all these arbitrary standards and embrace liberty." This is, logically rendered, "Let us not decide what is good, but let it be considered good not to decide it." He says, "Away with your old moral formulae; I am for progress," This, logically stated, means, "Let us not settle what is good; but let us settle whether we are getting more of it." He says, "Neither in religion or morality, my friend, lie the hopes of the race, but in education." This, clearly expressed, means, "We cannot decide what is good, but let us give it to our children.[5]

I had to quote the entire paragraph because it's just too, well, good! Discussions of the good would get us into deep philosophical waters, but the good isn't merely what works; a lot of things work that are very bad. The point Chesterton is making is that progress became an end in itself, untethered to the purposes for which it aims. It is the telos of a thing that in classical thinking determined if it was good or not; hammers are good if they are used to drive nails into wood, but not if used to clean the kitchen floor. If we are going in the wrong direction, making progress isn't progress at all.

Means and the ends toward which they *should* aim were slowly decoupled, and thus progress turned into progressivism. Sure, there was much talk about noble ends in the early days, but in due course the progressive do-gooders saw themselves as capable of telling the people what was good for them, whether they liked it or not. C.S. Lewis saw this in full fruition in the middle of the twentieth century in a piece he wrote in 1959 titled, "Is Progress Possible? Willing Slaves of the Welfare State."[6] After two brutal world wars and the rise of Soviet communism, it was a relevant question even in a Western world that still had an abiding faith in "progress." He saw the real pernicious danger of progressivism (although he didn't use the term):

> The modern state exists not to protect our rights but to do us good or makes us good—anyway, to do something to us or to make us something. Hence the new name 'leaders' for those who were once 'rulers." We are less their subjects than their wards, pupils or domestic animals. There is nothing left of which we can say to them, 'Mind your own business.' Our whole lives *are* their business.[6]

He argues in typically persuasive Lewis fashion that in due course this would become an "omnicompetent global technocracy," of course all for our good because, "If we are to be mothered, mother must know best." The Covid tyranny wouldn't have surprised him at all; he may have wondered what took so long! However, Covid and many other things are in fact revealing the omni-*incompetence* of the global technocratic elite. In his 1983 book *Idols for Destruction*,

Herbert Schlossberg speaks to the inevitable failure of the progressive project (he uses the equivalent term, statism):

> Modern statism is the soured remnant of the Enlightenment idea of inevitable progress. This miserable wreckage, which once heralded joyfully the coming of the secular version of the kingdom of God, now hoarsely wheezes that if we worship it we shall receive salvation from extinction. The danger is not to be taken lightly.[7]

He rightly calls it a fierce and implacable enemy, and indeed it is, but as powerful as it is, like the progressivism that gave it birth, it has within its ultimately futile ambitions the seeds of its own destruction. God has already seen to it.

GLOBALISM: THE TOWER OF BABEL FOR THE TWENTY FIRST CENTURY

The story of the Tower of Babel in Genesis 11 is more relevant today than ever before in human history. The ruinous consequences of the concentration of power are now global in scale in a way worthy of the most ambitious science fiction. Being endemic to the human condition the danger and temptation is nothing new, as God warned us a very long time ago only 11 chapters into the Bible:

> Now the whole world had one language and a common speech. [2] As people moved eastward, they found a plain in Shinar and settled there.
>
> [3] They said to each other, "Come, let's make bricks and bake them thoroughly." They used brick instead of

stone, and tar for mortar. ⁴ Then they said, "Come, let us build ourselves a city, with a tower that reaches to the heavens, so that we may make a name for ourselves; otherwise we will be scattered over the face of the whole earth."

⁵ But the Lord came down to see the city and the tower the people were building. ⁶ The Lord said, "If as one people speaking the same language they have begun to do this, then nothing they plan to do will be impossible for them. ⁷ Come, let us go down and confuse their language so they will not understand each other."

⁸ So the Lord scattered them from there over all the earth, and they stopped building the city. ⁹ That is why it was called Babel—because there the Lord confused the language of the whole world. From there the Lord scattered them over the face of the whole earth.

To put a fine biblical point on it, the societal concentration of power is satanic and evil, inevitably leading to tyranny. History makes that clear, but with the rise of modern technology a modern Babel is an existential threat as it has never been in history, and in that lies our hope of victory. I bet you didn't see that sentence coming! Let me explain.

The temptation to this concentration of power goes back even further to the serpent's temptation to Eve in Genesis 3 that if she just listened to him and ate the fruit of the tree of the knowledge of good and evil, she would "be like God, knowing good and evil." I've mentioned the word hubris several times thus far, and hubris is part of the genetic makeup of sinful human beings—we *all* want to "be like God." This is expressed in an infinite number of sinfully creative ways in each one of us, but it's always the bottom line of our rebellion against God; *we* want to call the shots, *we* want to determine what is good and evil. That hasn't worked out so well for the human race, but it doesn't stop us from trying.

Hubris, however, is more important for my purposes than just the technical definition of an overweening pride or excessive self-confidence. The concept goes back to ancient Greece, and this explanation at merriam-webster. com is illuminating:

> English picked up both the concept of hubris and the term for that particular brand of cockiness from the ancient Greeks, who considered hubris a dangerous character flaw capable of provoking the wrath of the gods. In classical Greek tragedy, hubris was often a fatal shortcoming that brought about the fall of the tragic hero. Typically, overconfidence led the hero to attempt to overstep the boundaries of human limitations and assume a godlike status, and the gods inevitably humbled the offender with a sharp reminder of their mortality.

Which leads us to another word the ancient Greeks used to explain this inevitable downfall, nemesis. More than an enemy or antagonist as we would typically use it today, it came into English meaning retributive justice, or getting what you deserve. Merriam-webster.com is again helpful in its description of the inevitable outcome of hubris:

> Nemesis was the Greek goddess of vengeance, a deity who doled out rewards for noble acts and punishment for evil ones. The Greeks believed that Nemesis didn't

always punish an offender immediately but might wait generations to avenge a crime.

When you put human beings together a la Babel, the hubris goes off the charts and leads inevitably and in due course to nemesis. This is a simple observation about human nature and existence, and the Greeks were very good at that. It is also biblical because it's the way God made the universe and how He interacts with man, the pinnacle of His creation. We see this in the story of Babel. God says about the builders that if He doesn't stop them, then "nothing they plan to do will be impossible for them." The story as metaphor is a fact of historical reality: man will not be allowed, in the vernacular, to pull it off, ever. We can't know the historical details of the actual city and tower of Babel, but the redemptive-historical meaning goes far beyond what happened there.

Fallen sinful man is a stubborn creature, and even though he is always frustrated in his god- and Babel-like ambitions, he will never stop trying to concentrate power. History, fortunately, makes clear the futility of every such endeavor, and the twenty-first century globalist movement will endure the same failure. God will always metaphorically confuse their language and scatter them over the face of the whole earth to make sure of it. This is more than just an observation of human nature and history. God has given us bread-crumbs throughout redemptive history that we might find our way back to Him, and have confidence that in the midst of evil the righteousness of God's heavenly kingdom rule will ultimately triumph. And when I speak of redemptive history, I'm not just speaking of that found in our Bibles as the phrase is commonly used, but also in reference to "the last days" after Christ rose from dead and he poured out the Holy Spirit at Pentecost. We will discuss the theological foundations for such a perspective and the confidence and optimism it brings in the final chapter.

IF NOT THE CONCENTRATION OF POWER, THEN WHAT?

Good question. The lesson of the tower of Babel is that concentrations of power must *always* be resisted in society, but what then is the alternative that works against this natural human tendency? In a word, liberty. Liberty was what America's founding generation believed was worth going to war for against the mightiest empire the world had ever known. To our Founders, however, that word meant something entirely different than it means to most Americans today. Never in their minds would it mean the license to do whatever someone wants. Such an idea was antithetical to true liberty, what some call ordered liberty, but that is a redundancy. Liberty, to be true liberty, must always be ordered. In our time though, it's come to be synonymous with the word *choice*, especially among libertarians and liberals. There is no more sacrosanct word among modern Americans than choice, but unlimited choice is a recipe for disaster at every level, personal, familial, societal. Our choices must always be constrained at each of these levels if we are to have true human flourishing. That we don't is an indication the true conception of liberty has been completely lost by many Americans.

In his magisterial work *Liberty and Freedom,* Historian David Hackett Fischer explores the historical development of these two different concepts and words. In the ancient world, both words "entailed obligations and responsibilities." To take them to mean that we should be able to choose whatever we want in life is a distortion of their true meaning. He writes:

In modern America too many people have forgotten this side of our inheritance. They think of liberty as license without responsibility, and freedom as entitlement without obligation. To think this way in the modern world is to remember only half of these ancient traditions.[8]

The history of Christian Western civilization is the slow outworking of these blessings in God's providence, most clearly seen in the centuries-long development of English common law and constitutionalism and reaching its apex in the founding of America by British subjects. Unfortunately, most Christians, like most Americans, are ignorant of this history and don't fully understand or appreciate this improbable development and what it took given sinful human nature. Knowing man's Babel-like tendencies makes this an enormous achievement in the history of the world, and completely unique. That uniqueness tells us something of its value, and why the founding generation was willing to commit their lives, their fortunes, and their sacred honor for the cause of liberty. It seems apparent to me that too few Christians appreciate the freedom and liberty bequeathed to us by the Founders.

Patriot Patrick Henry gave a memorable speech to the Second Virginia Convention in March 1775 presenting resolutions to raise and establish a militia and put Virginia in a posture of defense. He declares they are "engaged in a great and arduous struggle for liberty" and spoke of the millions of people "armed in the holy cause of liberty." He ended the speech to his fellow patriots with these resounding words that have echoed down through the ages:

What is it that gentlemen wish? What would they have? Is life so dear, or peace so sweet, as to be purchased at the price of chains and slavery? Forbid it, Almighty God! I know not what course others may take; but as for me, give me liberty or give me death!

These words are anachronistic and completely foreign to modern Americans who think of liberty as mere choice. They believe liberty is good as far as it goes, but they are not so sure it's worth dying for. We also take liberty for granted as much as the air we breathe. We wake up in the morning and it's just there. We don't ask how it got there; we just breathe. To the founding generation liberty would never have been taken for granted, realizing how precious and worthwhile it was because it was so rare.

Given its rarity, Christians above all people should be the most appreciative of what liberty and freedom mean for the advancing of God's kingdom, the propagation of the gospel and the building of Christ's church. I've found over my four plus decades as a Christian that most Christians appreciate what liberty means for the worship of God in public and church settings. I've heard many prayers of thanksgiving for the freedoms we have to worship that are not found in communist or Muslim countries. Unfortunately, because Christians tend to live their lives in what Frances Schaeffer referred to as a two-story reality, nature and grace, the spiritual and the temporal, the secular and the sacred, they tend not to appreciate what liberty means for advancement of God's kingdom in American culture and society. This is apparent in how few Christians see civic engagement as a priority specifically for Christian spiritual reasons. In other words, because we are Christians it is for Christian reasons we are to bring our influence to bear upon the society in which we live.

Sadly, prior to the compromised 2020 election, I was as much to blame as anyone. Growing up in California and becoming a conservative in the early 1980s, I dove into political action having been influenced by Francis Schaeffer. I was soon disillusioned by the cynicism I saw in the Republican Party. They thought we "social conservatives" were a dying and fractious breed who would ruin the appeal of the party to "normal" Americans. That hasn't worked out so well for the Republican Party of California which has zero political power in the state. Becoming disenchanted with politics, I figured I would just vote for the right person, and that would take care of my obligation to civic duty. That didn't work out so well either, or I wouldn't be writing this book! When the Internet came along, I started a blog in 2004, and thought that surely meant I was serious about changing things— then Trump. But it wasn't until after four years of Trump Derangement Syndrome, and the weaponization of the deep state against him, including Covid, that I finally woke up to my responsibility.

As I mentioned previously, I found Steve Bannon's *War Room*. His affirmation of our agency, that we have the ability and power to change things, resonated with me. To do that he consistently affirms change takes action, action, action! And for the first time in my adult life after that initial foray into politics when I was green and ignorant, I had hope that things could change in the direction of the founding principles of our country. It finally occurred to me that the first three words of the second most important of our founding documents, the Constitution, begin with the words, "*We the people* of the United States, in order to form a more perfect union..." For decades I thought it was other people's responsibility to do that, but I was wrong. It is mine. America is a self-governing republic, and if we don't insist on governing ourselves, then we will be governed by others, and often against our will.

WHAT WE FIGHT AGAINST IN DEFENSE OF OUR LIBERTY

The purpose of this chapter is not to identify all the specific ways our liberty is being threatened. There are bountiful resources that have done that in detail, both in books and on the Internet, but it is important to identify where those Babel-like tendencies are most threatening to our way of life. The threat of globalism is the macro picture, but that is the logical outgrowth of what happens on a state and national level. The paradigm shift, top down not bottom up, is a fundamental and dangerous reversal from the conception of the founders of America as a self-governing republic.

This change in orientation came with the rise of progressivism we discussed earlier and brought with it the rise of the administrative state. Prior to Donald Trump's presidency, I don't remember ever having heard that phrase, but now the danger is well known and often discussed. The New Deal, President Roosevelt's response to the Great Depression, began the vast growth of American government. Later, Lyndon Johnson's Great Society cemented the welfare state in public policy and in the minds of Americans as the normal state of things. The bureaucracy needed to support this welfare state grew as government revenue grew and took on a life of its own. The key feature of the administrative state is that it is not accountable to the people through its elected representatives. This is as much the fault of congress as the bureaucrats, but it is something that can no longer be ignored.

Next on the enemies list is globalism, which, thankfully, has become a bad word among right thinking Americans. It wasn't always that way. Many of us bought into the alure of globalism in the early 1990s when then President George H.W. Bush announced the coming of a "new world order" considering the fall of the Berlin Wall and the Soviet Union. The growth in international trade agreements in the Clinton years gave way to George W. Bush and both political parties supporting China becoming a member of the World Trade Organization. Everyone thought economic liberalization would lead to political liberalization in China, but those turned out to be naïve hopes. I'm ashamed to say I was among many who thought saving 30 cents on something at Walmart was worth shipping American manufacturing jobs overseas. It wasn't until Trump that I first questioned the benign promise of globalism even as it had already decimated communities throughout middle America.

Globalism is nothing new, although I'm not referring to the Tower of Babel. In 1971, Gary Allen wrote a book titled, *None Dare Call It Conspiracy*, in which he argued that both parties were in on a conspiracy to build a World Government. This was driven by organizations like the Council on Foreign Relations and international bankers. In the twenty-first century the same spirit of centralization is driven by billionaires like George Soros and Bill Gates and supported by organizations like the World Economic Forum (WEF). Some call it the spirit of Davos after the city in Switzerland where the world's richest oligarchs and policymakers meet every year to discuss the newest iteration of the technocratic "new world order." I heard Russell Brand say something brilliant in this regard: "There's no need for conspiracy when there's a convergence of interests." Mark Mitchell in his book, *Plutocratic Socialism*, explains the dangers of big business and big government, and how they feed off one another, the convergence Brand was talking about:

It is essential that we recognize an oft overlooked fact: economic centralization and political centralization feed off one another. Far from being antagonistic, they are natural allies. The history of the twentieth century shows that the massive regulatory state emerged with the explosive growth of corporate capitalism.

While the left now loves big business because it advances their woke agenda, conservatives have been slow to realize the threat it poses. As Mitchell adds, "It is essential to recognize that concentrations of power in any form are a threat to liberty."[9]

It is to the blessing of liberty and how it developed in Western Christian civilization that we turn next.

CHAPTER 10

THE STORY OF AN UNLIKELY CHRISTIAN WESTERN CIVILIZATION

From a merely human perspective Christian Western civilization shouldn't have happened. The odds of a ragtag crew of manual laborers in a small corner of the Roman Empire eventually turning the world upside down, or should we say right side up, were as close to zero as it possibly gets. From God's perspective, it was inevitable, baked into the salvific cake. The entire life, death, resurrection, and ascension of Jesus to the right hand of God was *the* inflection point in human history. Literally everything changed, only it didn't look like it, at all. For our purposes, we are going to look at a specific moment in Jesus' ministry where we witness an encounter with mustard seed significance (Matt. 13:31-32).

Jesus is confronted by his enemies (Matt. 22, Mark 12, Luke 20) with what they thought was a question that would land him in hot water with the Jews and Romans; there should have been no third option. Jesus' reply was completely unexpected. They asked if the Jews should pay tax to Caesar knowing if he said yes, he would be condemned by Jews, and if no, by Roman authorities. It was one or the other, they thought. But Jesus surprised them by asking whose likeness and inscription was on the coin, which he obviously knew. When they told him Caesar's, he replied: "Render to Caesar the things that are Caesar's, and to God the things that are God's." Thus, political reality changed forever in the Western world. Yes, it took the slow outworking of this principle for almost eighteen hundred years to finally see what the full fruition of this principle would look like in America's founding, but it started that day.

GOD AND CAESAR

At the time there was no *and*, only Caesar—all things belonged to Caesar. This was true in the Roman Empire, as well as in every other empire on earth whatever the ruler was called. Power ruled, might made right; everyone else would either submit or die. Now Jesus comes along and has the temerity to suggest the ruler must share his rule with God. This was radical, world changing radical, *if* Jesus was in fact who He claimed to be—He was and is. Christian Western Civilization is a direct result of the proclamation of the early church that Jesus is Lord, and Caesar is not.

First, Jesus is saying we have certain obligations to temporal rulers, be they Caesars, kings, presidents, or those in any position of civil authority. However, He is also saying something nobody prior had ever said: there are limits to rulers' power, and the things of God do not belong to them. We will discuss the concept of sphere sovereignty in the next chapter, but Jesus put strict limits on political power by limiting the sphere of political sovereignty. Such an idea was inconceivable in the ancient pagan world. After all, Alexander the Great's teacher, Aristotle, didn't exactly turn him into a Democrat. Yes, Aristotle thought despotism was bad, whether it was the rule of one (monarchy turns into tyranny), a small number of rulers (aristocracy turns into oligarchy), or rule by the many, democracy (a polity turns into the tyranny of 51%). What he didn't have was a transcendent authority in which to ground his arguments for the just state of limited powers. While Aristotle was one of the most brilliant men ever to live, human reason alone can only get us so far. Revelation was required to tell Caesar, hands off! The seed of this principle was planted by Jesus, and we'll see how the tree of liberty coming from it grew very slowly, but surely, as the story progresses.

Without the God of Judaism and Christianity, Israel's covenant God Yahweh revealed in Christ, tyranny is inevitable. Without God, if all we are is lucky dirt, then might makes right; morality is preference like preferring chocolate over vanilla ice cream. The logic of the "will to power" in a merely material world is irrefutable and inevitable. Why shouldn't the one with the biggest gun, or the biggest army, determine what is right and wrong? The pagan gods offered no defense against this logic because they were basically human beings with more power, which is an especially toxic brew. Ultimately, as we've discussed previously about the myth of neutrality, politics is religious in nature, and for a very long time in Western culture there has been a war between two mutually exclusive worldview systems, paganism (its current iteration is secularism) versus Christianity. This worldview war is nothing new.

CHRISTIANITY VERSES PAGANISM

The war against paganism in redemptive history also goes back a very long way. This is the same worldview war we fight today—it only looks more sophisticated.

The Bible doesn't inform us how long it was from Babel (Gen. 11) to God calling Abram out of Ur of the Chaldeans, but it's only one chapter. In the first verses of Genesis 12, the Lord says to Abram: "Go from your country, your people and your father's household to the land I will show you," and "all the peoples on earth will be blessed through you." That land was Canaan and it encompassed modern day Israel and surrounding lands. The blessing would eventually encompass the entire world starting with God developing a covenant relationship with Abram (Gen. 15). The Lord declared through a covenant ceremony that He would be responsible for both sides of the agreement making it a legally binding contract in the ancient world. In Genesis 3, the Lord had promised the seed of the woman would bruise or strike the serpent's head, and we see here the beginnings of the fulfillment of that promise. Amid a heathen world, God would use one man to create a people for Himself. Subsequently this people would defeat the dominant pagan religions of the ancient world to create a modern world where the knowledge of God would one day stretch throughout the earth.

In the ensuing 2000 years, God's plans didn't appear to be progressing much. After His promises to Abram in Genesis 12 and 15, then confirming His covenant in the sign of circumcision (17) and changing his name to Abraham (means father of many), God put him through the ultimate test with Isaac (22). When Abraham passed the test, the Lord confirmed His promise yet again:

> [17] I will surely bless you and make your descendants as numerous as the stars in the sky and as the sand on the seashore. Your descendants will take possession of the cities of their enemies, [18] and through your

offspring all nations on earth will be blessed, because you have obeyed me."

The entire history of Israel is the story of one battle after another in this religious i.e., worldview, war. From the beginning of Israel's identity as a people, they vacillate between embracing the idolatry and paganism of the surrounding nations, or Yahweh and the true worship of God. The story seems to end without an ending in the last book of the Old Testament, Malachi, but it points forward to the messenger of the one who would bring ultimate victory over the enemies of God's people. In Malachi 3:1 we are introduced to Yahweh's messenger:

> "I will send my messenger, who will prepare the way before me. Then suddenly the Lord you are seeking will come to his temple; the messenger of the covenant, whom you desire, will come," says the Lord Almighty.

Four hundred years later John the Baptist turned out to be the messenger, and Malachi tells us this will be the beginning of something big, a momentous salvific moment in the history of redemption:

> 5 "See, I will send the prophet Elijah to you before that great and dreadful day of the Lord comes. 6 He will turn the hearts of the parents to their children, and the hearts of the children to their parents; or else I will come and strike the land with total destruction."

And Jesus, as He does in His often-cryptic way, confirms this in Matthew 11:

¹⁴ And if you are willing to accept it, he is the Elijah who was to come. ¹⁵ Whoever has ears, let them hear.

At the time Jesus appeared on the scene, victory over God's enemies certainly didn't appear anywhere on the horizon. Israel was a small backwater province in an obscure corner of the Roman Empire, the Romans being only their latest oppressors. They certainly didn't resemble the stars in the sky or the sand on the seashore promised to Abraham two thousand years previously.

Jesus' disciples were convinced He was the long-awaited Messiah who would fulfill God's covenant promise and give His people victory over their enemies, finally ushering in God's kingdom reign on earth. Prior to the resurrection, they didn't realize the Messiah's immediate concerns were not geopolitical, but rather saving His people from their sins (Matt. 1:21). When Jesus was crucified on a cross, hung on a tree indicating he was under God's curse (Deut. 21:23, Gal. 3:13), they *knew* He could not be their long-awaited Messiah—until the third day. Jesus then explained to them how the entire Old Testament is about Him (Luke 24), which would include the promise to multiply Abraham's seed beyond human ability to count. The geopolitical and cultural implications would take time to become apparent as God's kingdom advanced and the church grew like leaven in a very large batch of dough (Matt. 13:31–35).

The Apostles and the New Testament Church also didn't have geopolitics and culture on their minds because they expected Jesus to come back within their lifetimes. We see in Acts and the Epistles how this new Christian faith would influence their actions toward the political powers of the day, but it wouldn't be until well into the second century when it became apparent Jesus might not be coming back soon after all. Christian thinkers would need to explore more fully the implications of Christianity for society.

This became imperative when, against all expectations, Constantine converted to Christianity in the early fourth century, and Christianity was declared the official religion of the Roman Empire in 380 AD by Emperor Theodosius I. The implications for Christianity on society became even more imperative when in the early fifth century the Goths sacked Rome and overran the Roman Empire. The pagans blamed the Christians and their strange religion for angering the gods and bringing the downfall of the Empire. A robust defense of Christianity was required, and Augustine, the great Bishop of Hippo (northern Africa), mounted one in his erudite tome, *The City of God*. This influential work would reverberate down through the ages as Christians realized there were no easy answers to the questions posed by those who inhabited a heavenly city and how they would engage with the earthly city. It seemed the pagans, though, would again be the dominant force in Europe, and God's promise to Abraham delayed yet again.

HOW THE IRISH SAVED CHRISTIAN WESTERN CIVILIZATION

Scholars influenced by Enlightenment bias used to call the period from the collapse of Roman civilization in the fifth century to the Renaissance in the thirteenth the "Dark Ages," when all classical learning and the treasures of the ancient world supposedly disappeared from the West. Now commonly referred to as the Middle Ages, to a large degree, Christian monks and scribes on the British Isles during this time kept knowledge of the ancient world alive, including Judaism and Christianity. The title of this section comes from a wonderful book by Thomas Cahill called, *How the Irish Saved Civilization.* I added Christian and Western because what made modern civilization possible as well as "Western" was the specifically Christian faith in spiritual and the eventual physical battle against the barbarian hoards from the north. The pagan worldview and religion would be at war with this budding civilization for centuries as the leaven and mustard seed of God's kingdom would eventually defeat these ancient versions of paganism.

As I briefly relate some of the history of the Middle Ages, keep in mind chapter three and the Christian theology of history: God's providence directs all things to His appointed ends in due course. Christianity and coincidence are mutually exclusive categories. None of this is by chance.

Each year on March 17, the Western world celebrates St. Patrick's Day, and maybe one in a million people know why. I didn't fully know the story of Patrick and his true significance until I read Cahill's book. His life was the domino God pushed to begin the process of growing Christian influence in the West, and eventually the world. Patrick lived during the fifth century and was born in modern England at the end of Roman Rule in Britain. At sixteen he was captured by Irish pirates and brought to Ireland where he spent six years in captivity as a shepherd and converted to Christianity. He escaped, made it back to Britain, and eventually reunited with his family. There he grew in the knowledge of his faith and had a vision in a dream where he believed God was calling him to return to Ireland as what today we would call a missionary, probably the first since the Apostles. Before he left, he was ordained as a priest and bishop so his ministry would be sanctioned by the church. According to Cahill, Patrick:

In his last years could probably look out over an Ireland transformed by his teaching. According to tradition, at least, he established bishops throughout northern, central, and eastern Ireland... With the Irish—even with the kings—he succeeded beyond measure. Within his lifetime or soon after his death, the Irish slave trade came to a halt, and other forms of violence, such as murder and intertribal warfare, decreased.[1]

In other words, God's promises to Abraham are starting not only to be fulfilled in the souls of people, but in how they lived in society.

Learning and the spread of knowledge reflected a significant contrast between pagan and Christian civilization after Rome. When the heathen hoards poured in from the north, they not only brought with them violence, but ignorance, and the destruction of learning, libraries burned, and books turned to dust. These were not your learned classical pagans of Rome and Greece, a world destroyed with Rome. The elite, leisured, learned class which made learning possible would soon cease to exist, and the books they once paid to have copied by scribes began to disappear. Over time, Patrick's influence would also bring the light of learning into a Europe enveloped in pagan darkness. For the next two hundred years people from all over Ireland, soon England, and then from Europe came to learn from the monks inspired by Patrick. As monasteries developed into little university towns, Cahill tells the story of scribes who:

> took up the great labor of copying all of western literature—everything they could lay their hands on. These scribes then served as the conduits through

which the Greco-Roman and Judeo-Christian cultures were transmitted to the tribes of Europe . . . Without the service of the Scribes, everything that happened subsequently would have been unthinkable.[2]

Except it wasn't "unthinkable" to Almighty God! This knowledge will bring us to our next glimpse of the inexorable spread of Christendom, and a story of God's providence every bit as seemingly against the odds as Patrick's.

HOW KING ALFRED THE GREAT
SAVED WHAT PATRICK STARTED

Though Patrick's influence was felt far and wide, the heathen barbarians were relentless, which moves us forward to the ninth century and the reign of King Alfred the Great of England (Wessex) from 871-899. Alfred aspired to establish a Christian-united England under one king. He's the only king in English history with the appellation Great attached to his name because he started the process to unite England under the law of God. Several years ago, my daughter told me about a Netflix series called *The Last Kingdom* (i.e., Wessex). I was quickly hooked, not only because it was well done, but also because I knew absolutely nothing about the history portrayed on the screen. I was amazed to learn Christian Western civilization as we know it hung by a thread during Alfred's reign, and from a human perspective, a thread might be overestimating the odds.

In Winston Churchill's *A History of the English-Speaking Peoples, The Birth of Britain*, he calls the period from the late 800s to 1050, the Viking Age, referring to it as a "murderous struggle."[3] There was no such thing as Viking people. The reference is something like calling them pirates. The Danes were representative and were Alfred's primary adversaries, but Vikings were Scandinavian seafaring warriors who left their homelands during these years in search of a better life on an Island seeming to promise it. Since the time of Patrick, the Christian church had become the sole haven of learning and knowledge, something that seemed to amuse and perplex the Vikings, at least according to the portrayal in *The Last Kingdom*. I think they got it right.

One of my favorite scenes is in season one when Alfred and the Danish leaders Guthrum and Ubba are negotiating. They ask Alfred what the transcribers are writing, and he says, "They are writing what we speak." He adds, "They are writing history. We are here creating history. People will read of this very meeting." The heathens didn't write or create history. They also ask why he seeks peace, and he says, "It is the Christian in me, the will of my God." Ubba wants to talk of the gods, and Alfred replies firmly, "God, there is only one." This encounter is a microcosm of two mutually exclusive forces, the two worldviews we've surveyed for almost 3,000 years now, and only one could be victorious. Christianity would bring learning and peace, the rule of law, and the advance of God's kingdom in the world, or the pagans would bring a bloody world of arbitrary power none of us would want to live in.

Tom Holland reminds us, "So profound has been the impact of Christianity on the development of Western civilization that it has come to be hidden from view."[4] Because of secular progressive education, the influence of Christianity to most people is invisible. Speaking of the ancient world, Holland writes what could also apply to the heathen Vikings trying to take England from the Christians:

> The Greeks, when they captured a city, had licensed rape as a reward for valor. The Romans had stocked

their households with young boys and girls, and used them as they pleased. Everyone in antiquity had taken for granted that infanticide was perfectly legitimate; that to turn the other cheek was folly; that "Nature has given the weak to be slaves."[5]

Without the eyes of faith, which Alfred had in abundance, England could very easily have become Daneland, and heathen with paganism the dominant religion. It was as close, as I said, as a thread.

Wessex was the last Anglo-Saxon kingdom not to fall to the Vikings. By 875, they decided Alfred and Wessex would be next, the last kingdom in Britain yielding to the inevitable onslaught to come. Unlike the Scandinavians, Alfred didn't have a large professional standing army to call on, but mostly depended on militias called fyrds, farmers who fought, then went back to their farms. Guthrum looked to have the advantage, Wessex would fall, and Christian England lost to history. Prepared to deliver the final blow to Alfred, Ubba, another Scandinavian warlord king, sailed south with many Viking ships and many thousands of warriors to join Guthrum west of Wessex.

In one of the great "coincidences" of Christian Western history, a freak storm destroyed the fleet and Guthrum retreated to the north. According to Churchill:

> A hundred and twenty ships were sunk, and upwards of five thousand of these perjured marauders perished as they deserved. Thus the whole careful plan fell to pieces...[6]

Alfred believed the storm was divine judgment on the heathens, but they were not done. In early 878, Wessex, during a surprise attack, suffered a defeat at the hand of Guthrum and the Danes. Alfred fled, hiding for several months as a fugitive in marshlands with just a few hundred followers, hardly anyone in Wessex even knowing if he was still alive. The marshlands ended up saving not only Alfred, but Christian England from paganism as well.

When news went out in Wessex that Alfred was indeed still alive, all his fighting men came back for what turned out to be a culminating battle for Alfred and Christian England at Ethandun (now Edington). We might say this was Alfred's last stand. In *The Last Kingdom* there is a wonderful scene as the warriors of Wessex and the heathens face each other ready for battle. Alfred says, "If the heathens win, then Christ is defeated. The swords of England, of Wessex, have answered the call." Christ was not defeated, and Christian England saved, as was arguably Christian Western civilization. If the heathens had won, and they easily could have, there would have been no Magna Carta, no Glorious Revolution, no Pilgrims or Puritans, or America. It was Alfred who conceived and accomplished the beginnings of a united Christian England. His grandson, Athelstan, finished the work and would be known as "King of the English."

Alfred did not treat his victory over Guthrum like it would have been done to him and Wessex if the pagans had won. He could have wiped out the Danes or enslaved them, but as Churchill says, "Alfred meant to make a lasting peace with Gurthrum,"[7] something inconceivable to the heathens if they were victorious, but conceivable to a ruler who follows the Prince of Peace. As a condition of that peace, Alfred insisted Guthrum, along with his leading men, be baptized and become a Christian, which he did, with Alfred as his godfather. He adopted the Christian name Aethelstan

THE STORY OF AN UNLIKELY CHRISTIAN WESTERN

and ruled peacefully as a Christian king in East Anglia for ten years.

MAGNA CARTA TO THE GLORIOUS REVOLUTION AND THE RULE OF LAW

The next period in English history we'll look at in the never-ending war against the centralizing spirit of Babel is Magna Carta (1215) to the Glorious Revolution (1688). Alfred was given the appellation Great for many reasons. Not only was he a warrior king who saved Christian England from the heathen hordes, but he was also a scholar king in ways almost unimaginable after the fall of Rome. In addition to promoting scholarship and general learning among the people, he was committed to the reign of Christ and the rule of God's law over England. His vision was to establish a Christian England. His most important accomplishment to this end was building on previous kings to establish his Law Code built on the foundation of the Ten Commandments, and thus beginning the slow growth of English common law. We would recognize this today as the practice of law in courts, "a system for identifying principles and apply-ing them to novel factual contexts."[8] Understanding this development is crucial in the war against Babel because the only thing keeping power from absolutizing (the cen-tralizing spirit) is the rule of law, something nonexistent anywhere in the world until it's development in England. Magna Carta, also called the Great Charter, is a milestone in Christian Western civilization and English constitutional history. Briefly explaining the context will help us under-stand why it is so important.

Prior to this time there were no legal limits on the authority of the sovereign. What the king decreed was law.

This power was something kings were loath to relinquish, but in due course they did. Simply, the Great Charter enumerated English liberties granted by King John on June 15, 1215, under threat of civil war from the barons, or nobility. According to Churchill:

> The leaders of the barons in 1215 groped in the dim light towards a fundamental principle. Government must henceforward mean something more than the arbitrary rule of any man, and custom and the law must stand even above the king... The Charter became in the process of time an enduring witness that the power of the crown was not absolute.[9]

For a variety of reasons, the king felt like he had to give way in this power struggle. The Charter was signed, and reissued with alterations in 1216, 1217, and 1225. By declaring the sovereign to be subject to the rule of law and documenting the liberties held by "free men," Magna Carta provided the foundation for individual rights in English law. The specific clauses are not what is important about the Charter, but one, Clause 39, gives an indication of just how revolutionary this document was in establishing true justice in Christian Western civilization:

> No free man shall be arrested or imprisoned or disseised or outlawed or exiled or in any way victimised, neither will we attack him or send anyone to attack him, except by the lawful judgment of his peers or by the law of the land.

This is remarkable when you realize in the thousands of years of recorded history prior to this fulcrum moment, the will to power of one man, or a small group of men, was law. Might made right. According to Ryan Alford:

> In exchange for the taxes necessary to wage the Hundred Year's War, Edward III (1312-1377) confirmed the Charter no less than fifteen times, a process that was motivated by "a desire to get the king's acknowledgment in general that he was bound by law." By the end of Edward III's reign, the principle of legality was no longer disputable largely due to his repeated reaffirmations and amplifications of Magna Carta.[10]

Alford further states it was commonly assumed that "the Great Charter's protections applied to everyone regardless of station, and that the rights it established were by this time considered absolute and non-derogable."[11] A non-derogable right is one whose infringement is not justified under any circumstances, and analogous to the unalienable rights of America's Declaration. Yoram Hazony tells us this distinct understanding of rights and limitations on the king's power is in contrast with the Holy Roman Empire and with France, which were governed by Roman law, and therefore by the maxim that "what pleases the prince has the force of law," thus allowing absolute government.[12]

Nonetheless, English kings would not give up their power easily.

When Queen Elizabeth I died in 1603, the era of the Tudor monarchy ended, and King James I of Scotland (1566-1625) who succeeded her ushered in the bumpy reign of the Stuarts. We might say James was not a big fan of Magna Carta, believing fervently the absolute right of kings was a divine right, and "the laws are the king's freely given gift, which he can choose to make or revoke as he pleases."[13] This flew in the face of the intellectual currents of the time. Samuel Rutherford (1600-1661), a Scottish Presbyterian pastor, theologian, and political theorist, published the popular and influential book *Lex Rex, or The Law and the Prince*, in 1644. Arguing in a sense that the law is king, that even the king is subject to the law, the book was a hammer blow against the king and state's claims for absolute power. After he died, it was publicly burned.

During James' reign parliament would become increasingly self-assertive, while his son Charles I (1600-1649) endured a civil war with parliament leading to his execution. Now without a king, England experimented with a reign of parliament under Puritan Oliver Cromwell (1599-1658) called the Commonwealth of England, Scotland and Ireland or Protectorate which lasted until 1660. A government in Medieval Europe without monarchy was never going to be a long-term solution, and this government proved an unworkable solution. Then in a supreme act of historical irony, the same parliament that executed Charles I invited his son Charles II to the throne, known as the Restoration. While his reign was controversial with many disputes over the scope of his powers, the most serious rupture between the constitutionalists and the monarchy didn't happen until the ascension of his younger brother to the throne, James II in 1685.

It was the Catholic James who instigated the events leading to the Glorious Revolution and the end of the reign of the Stuarts. Most important was his reissue of the Declaration of Indulgence in April 1688 indicating the royal prerogative was going to be a regular feature of his reign. The Declaration itself affirmed an absolute monarchy while granting religious liberties to the King's subjects, but it also reaffirmed the King's "Sovereign Authority, Prerogative Royal and absolute power, which all our Subjects are to obey without Reserve." In June, a Catholic Prince of Wales and possible future king was born, and seven high-ranking members of parliament invited the Protestant William, a Dutch prince and his wife, Mary, to England. William landed in England with an army and James was captured, but later allowed to flee to France. In February 1689, Parliament offered the crown jointly to William and Mary, provided they accept the Bill of Rights, which "placed the royal prerogative and the monarchs themselves unambiguously under the law."[14] The change of dynasty creating a constitutional monarchy is what is known as the Glorious Revolution partly because it was bloodless.

This period of English history had a significant influence on America's Founders, but before we get there, we must briefly examine something all modern people take for granted, the nation-state. We will look at its historical development from a specifically Christian perspective, and how it too is integral in the never-ending war against the centralizing spirit of Babel.

CHAPTER 11

THE WESTPHALIAN NATION-STATE AND THE CHRISTIAN NATION

Another gift of Christian Western civilization is the nation-state. I wonder how many Americans know that the idea of a nation with identifiable sovereign borders is a relatively new phenomena in the history of the world. Prior to the seventeenth century, borders were determined by military power, and as power dynamics shifted among peoples, so did borders. This began to change in the seventeenth century as the result of a European peace treaty. According to Wikipedia:

> The Westphalian system is a principle in international law that each state has exclusive sovereignty over its territory. The principle underlies the modern international system of sovereign states... every state, no matter how large or small, has an equal right to sovereignty. Political scientists have traced the concept to the Peace of Westphalia (1648), which ended the Thirty Years' War (1618–1648) and Eighty Years' War (1568–1648).

So taken for granted by most people, it is assumed to be the natural order of things—it is not. The reason might be obvious by now if you've read this far: Babel. This sinful dynamic of reality has come down to us in the famous aphorism of Lord Acton:

> Power tends to corrupt, and absolute power corrupts absolutely. Great men are almost always bad men...

I would qualify this slightly: all men are bad. Christian theology teaches us, according to the Apostle Paul, that "all have sinned and fall short of the glory of God," and, "There is no one righteous, not even one." In the Calvinist or Reformed understanding of Christianity this is called total depravity, not as in everyone is as depraved or evil as they can be, but every part of every human being is corrupted by sin. I would further qualify this: power doesn't just tend to corrupt but is inherently corrupting. Other sinful human tendencies do not have the capability to destroy entire civilizations like power in the hands of a Stalin, Hitler, or Mao. Babel teaches us that hubris will always tend to make people consolidate power to unbiblical tyrannical ends unless they are countered with forces that limit their power, something America's Founders understood better than any thinkers the world has ever known.

Because the nation-state is unnatural, it is fragile, and in our day is uniquely under assault by transnational globalist elites who see borders as inhibiting their Babel-like agenda. Put simply, nationalism is an obstacle to the goals of the globalist technocratic elite, the builders of a modern globalist babel. Given this natural sinful tendency to centralize and absolutize power, Christians are obligated to be nationalists, and need to recognize the satanic threat of globalism. In the last chapter I referenced Gary Allen's book, *None Dare Call It Conspiracy,* because at the time those who warned of the threat of globalism were called, you guessed it, conspiracy theorists. Now the globalists are in our faces with their World Economic Forums and annual soirees in places like Davos, Switzerland, where the rich and famous hobnob while discussing how to change the world ostensibly for our good, the worst form of tyranny.

THE CHARACTERISTICS OF A NATION

A nation is more than borders, much more. It is first a local experience because loyalty and commitment come from the bottom up: first the family, then the locality, town, or city, then the county, the state, and finally the nation. There is no further Christian obligation beyond that. I will address the concept of sphere sovereignty below, but the organic nature of the nation is described well by Stephen Wolfe:

> [T]he nation, properly understood, is a particular people with ties of affection that bind them to each other and their place of dwelling; and thus national-ism is the nation acting for its national good, which includes conversation of those ties of affection.[1]

Affection is the operative word. We can't have a real personal devotion and loyalty to an abstraction like a United Nations or a European Union. Affection is only possible with what we know in some measure personally, intimately. The neighbors we see every day, or the parents at school, or people in the grocery store, it is they with whom we develop a connection, not people on a screen on the other side of the world. This sense of peoplehood, if you will, is inevitable and necessary in a world full of nations. Yoram Hazony further defines nation as:

A number of tribes with a shared heritage, usually including a common language or religious traditions, and a past history of joining together against common enemies—characteristics that permit tribes so united to understand themselves as a community distinct from other such communities that are their neighbors.

He then defines nationalism as:

A principled standpoint that regards the world as governed best when nations are able to chart their own independent course, cultivating their own traditions and pursuing their own interests without interference.[2]

While obliterating these God-created connections and distinctions is ultimately impossible, globalists either ignore or denigrate such attachments because they stand in their way of global Utopia. As we discussed for the secular Utopian Marxist project these connections, starting with the family, must be destroyed. If the economic communists of the twentieth century couldn't pull this off with all the military might at their disposal, the cultural Marxists of the twenty-first in what is primarily an information war won't be able to either.

The push back against this drive to globalize the world began to manifest itself with Brexit, the movement in the UK to pull out of the European Union. The election to confirm England's exit from the EU was on June 23, 2016, but the debate had been going on for a while. Open borders, a globalist necessity, and mass immigration from non-European countries, much of it illegal, was a primary driver of Brexit and other nationalist movements through-out Europe. The two sides were predictable and were the precursor to the same dynamic leading to the very unlikely election of President Trump. The cultural elites, global-ists all, thought Brexit had no more chance of passing than Trump had of winning later in the year. They also thought British patriots were deplorables as Hillary Clinton infamously asserted about Trump's followers. It was the same patriotic nationalism that made the MAGA move-ment (Make America Great Again) possible. Trump rode this nationalist wave to power, the right man in the right place at the right time.

THE NECESSITY OF A CHRISTIAN NATION

I don't use the phrase "Christian nationalism" because of the anti-Christian baggage, but also because anytime an *ism* is added to a word it must be handled carefully. Without the baggage, if you're a Christian and you believe in nations (i.e., you're not a globalist), I contend you should be a Christian nationalist. The concept of the nation, or specific people groups, is an important biblical concept, the word being used well over 600 times. In fact, when Jesus gave what we've come to call the Great Commission to the eleven in Matthew 28, He told them to make disciples of all nations (ethnos in Greek), not a comparable Greek word for indi-viduals. In Acts 17 the Apostle Paul lays out the case for the God-ordained nature of nations:

> 26 From one man he made all the nations, that they should inhabit the whole earth; and he marked out their appointed times in history and the boundaries of their lands.

You can't get more biblically unequivocal than that! Further, if you accept my argument in the chapter on secularism about the myth of neutrality, you'll realize a religiously or morally neutral nation cannot exist. Unfortunately, many Christians still believe this myth at some level, and suspect a Christian nation is a synonym for theocracy. Of course, everything depends on what someone means by "theocracy," which we'll get to below.

This myth leads many Christians to mistakenly believe religious freedom means a type of pluralism where all faiths are equally welcome at a neutral public table with mutual respect and tolerance for all. A perfect example of this misconception comes from David French, a one-time conservative who became an implacable foe of Donald Trump (joining what came to be called the Never Trumpers). This quote comes from an article in the left-wing *Atlantic* magazine titled, "Pluralism Has Life Left in It Yet":

> The magic of the American republic is that it can create space for people who possess deeply different world views to live together, work together, and thrive together, even as they stay true to their different religious faiths and moral convictions.[3]

This magic world of America that French invents out of whole cloth never existed, because in God's created reality, currently fallen and chock full of sinners, such a pluralist Utopia does not and cannot exist. In fact, America was founded as a Protestant republic with shared biblical assumptions and the Bible as its foundational religious text. Most people don't realize, obviously including David French, that for the first approximately 170 years of America's history most states had anti-blasphemy and sabbath laws. Doesn't sound very magical or pluralistic to me!

What French and others like him seem to miss is that we are living in an era when America's (and the West's) established religion is secular progressivism, otherwise known as wokeness (i.e., cultural Marxism). It has its own anti-blasphemy laws, as we know all too well. There can be legal consequences, for example, for speaking any words perceived as racist or anti any so-called sexual minority. Vishal Mangalwadi states an unalterable fact of existence:

> Every civilization is tied together by a final source of authority that gives meaning and ultimate intellectual, moral, and social justification to its culture.[4]

He suggests there have been at least five sources of such authority in Western civilization, the current being "individualistic nihilism." Any society basing its ultimate source of authority on separate and isolated individuals, and their choices as the ultimate or highest good of existence, will in fact lead to nothingness(nihilism) and the despair and frustration associated with it. There is plenty of evidence of this. In 2022 almost 50,000 people committed suicide in America, a record. This won't surprise us when we see that the suicide rate for people between 15 and 24 years of age has tripled since the 1950s. We have the sacred choice of the individual as the final source of authority and the nihilism it creates to thank for these tragic statistics.

Every nation has some kind of religious establishment, some foundation upon which social order or disorder is based, and the consequences will naturally follow. As Christians we can either stick our heads in the sand and pretend neutrality exists or start thinking seriously and rigorously about what a Christian nation would look like. We can't know this with absolute certainty because God only gives us the broad contours of the blessings that righteousness brings to a nation. Every nation is different, but civic and cultural engagement is a necessity if this is to happen. This book, though, is primarily an assessment of the environment in which we find ourselves and an argument for the necessity of such a project.

The reason we are where we are, as previously discussed, is that Enlightenment rationalism bequeathed to us liberalism to one degree or another (a complicated discussion). Liberalism with the God of Scripture in Christ, largely because of the Puritans and the First Great awakening, gave us America; liberalism without Him gave us the French Revolution. There is no in between. Secularism will eventually allow no competitors in the public square. Americans were sold a bill of goods that once secularism pushed the God of the Bible off the public and cultural stage all would be sweetness and light. It hasn't turned out that way because it *never* could. Blessed is the nation whose God is the Lord, Scripture tells us, the nation that abandons Him, well, America circa 2024 is the result.

You may have already come to my conclusion. In the West we will either have Christian nations or secular nations, and secular nations will always tend to totalitarian because they have rejected the only true basis of liberty—the Bible, God's law, and word.

THE KINGDOM, THE CHURCH, AND THE NATION

Related to the issue of a Christian nation, is the problem of the modern confusion in conflating the Church with the kingdom of God. Until recently I believed the kingdom was the church, and the church was the kingdom. This is not true. The kingdom of God or heaven is God's rule or reign on earth brought by God's redeemed people, not by church bodies as such. It is also not just saved Christians who advance God's kingdom on earth, but saved Christians who apply their biblical and Christian worldview to every square inch of life, a la Abraham Kuyper who said:

> There is not a square inch in the whole domain of our human existence over which Christ, who is Sovereign overall, does not cry, Mine!"[5]

God's kingdom is also advanced by non-Christians who embrace Christian values and assumptions about the nature of reality and apply them. Worldviews have consequences, and our job as faithful Christians is to inculcate the Christian worldview into the culture, which is a people's beliefs externalized and applied. The ultimate goal is people imbibing a Christian worldview instead of the poison of the secular woke cultural Marxism they currently do. No culture, like its government, is worldview neutral.

When I started thinking about writing the book in early 2022, I struggled with what we as conservative and Evangelical Christians are trying to accomplish. What exactly is a Christian society or nation? What does such a thing look like? Is it fifty-one percent of the people being professing Christians? I was always frustrated because I knew intuitively what makes a nation Christian isn't just the number of Christians. I'm not sure there's ever been a time in Western history where the vast majority of people in the nations of Christendom were Christians, yet the people, Christian or not, considered themselves living in Christian nations. Most Christians seem to believe if we just convert enough people things will magically change for the better. It doesn't work that way.

Joseph Boot relates well how this kingdom-church confusion creates a false dilemma:

> Believers tend to think that they are confronted with a very restricted choice in these matters: either pursue a return to a form of the ecclesiastical culture of Christendom where power and authority over various cultural and political matters is restored to a particular church denomination, or accept that we now live in a post-Christian age where the only thing Christians can realistically hope for is being one of many interest groups in a diverse, multicultural society, perhaps with a seat at the table—a chair pulled out for us by a humanistic secular state now to be embraced as the norm for human society.[6]

As he indicates, the second view dominates modern Evangelicalism.

The problem, other than these not being the only two choices, and I would argue neither is the Christian choice, is that both lead to totalitarianism. Neither Christian nor pagan (i.e., secular) totalitarianism lead to good results as the historical evidence makes painfully clear. However, going beyond these two limiting choices we realize there are indeed only two *ultimate* choices—the rule of God or the rule of man, as I argued in the last chapter—God or paganism. It is abundantly clear how the latter works, but unfortunately there is an abundance of confusion about how the former would work in the modern world. The rule of God in a nation isn't difficult to understand, but ignorance and secular programming makes it so. Bringing such a reality to pass is another story.

The context of this discussion among Christians is often American exceptionalism or loving America and thinking it is the most exceptionally blessed country in the history of the world. What is especially to be avoided is thinking our nation is better than others, as if God has uniquely blessed America, which he most obviously has. Christians who have a problem with this warn us that America is not a theocracy like ancient Israel, but I don't know any Christian who believes it is. God, however, has a relationship to every country on earth, and blesses or curses those nations to the degree they look to Him as the ultimate governor and ruler of the nation.

Stephen Wolfe calls this "a nation with a Christian self-conception."[7] This makes it a war on two fronts, cultural and political. I realized some time ago just focusing on politics alone was a fool's errand. I overcompensated for a while thinking it was all about the culture which eventually trickles down to politics. It is, however, very much a two-way street—culture affects politics, and politics affects culture. But for most Evangelical Christians, once you get past the personal salvation of someone's soul and start talking about Christianizing the nation, they get nervous, and to the theocracy charge they go. We need to change that. A Christian nation has no choice but to be a theocracy, properly understood.

WHAT EXACTLY IS A THEOCRACY?

Which brings us to the meaning of this word that causes so much consternation. It is a question of great importance, so we must not rush past it. First, what does theocracy mean? It comes from a Greek compound word for God (theos) and rule (krateo) which doesn't sound so bad, right? If we're

Christians, all of reality is theocracy, but throughout history those acting in the name of God gave the term its tyrannical baggage. R.J. Rushdoony explains why theocracy is so often misunderstood:

> Theocracy is falsely assumed to be a take-over of government, imposing biblical law on an unwilling society. This presupposes statism which is the opposite of theocracy. Because modern people only understand power as government, they assume that's what we want.[8]

The key words are "imposing" and "unwilling." All secularists, be they religious or not, believe if we bring Christianity and God's law into the public square, we will be "imposing" our faith and its moral values on others. Believing this, skeptics of an ignorant type make the statement, "You can't legislate morality," which is like saying, you can't cook food; food is what you cook, as morality is what you legislate. The only issue is *whose* morality, and from whence it comes.

In fact, as we see clearly, the secular leftist state is tyrannically imposing its morality, the latest example being transgenderism where the state, by force of law, dictates that biological males must be allowed to compete in girls and women's sports and use women's bathrooms. Talk about "imposing" law on an "unwilling" society! Few people in Western societies are secular progressive absolutist woke leftists who believe sex is merely a social construct changeable at will, yet the woke have no problem imposing their policies on an unwilling society. That's the way it works—no neutrality, God's law or man's.[9] The difference is God's law, in James' words, is the "law of liberty" (1:25,

2:12). When Jesus proclaimed "liberty to the captives" in Luke 4:18 quoting Isaiah 61:1, He wasn't proclaiming liberty *from* the law of God, but the liberty coming from obedience to it. As the Apostle Paul states in I Timothy 1, "the law is good if used properly," and it "conforms to the gospel concerning the glory of the blessed God." The law and the gospel are not in any way at odds. God's law is always and everywhere for all time, a reflection of His being, and He calls all to obedience to it if they are to experience His blessing and true human flourishing.

As we discussed in the last chapter, the rule of law informed by God's law is a distinctly Christian notion against the will to power of paganism; because of it, liberty was established in Christian Western civilization. It's either God and liberty, or secularism leading to tyranny or anarchy, the logical conclusions of man's law without God. Critiquing rationalism, Yoram Hazony paints the mutually exclusive God or man picture:

> The fundamental incompatibility of Enlightenment rationalism with the God of Scripture had been made plain, and it has remained visible to anyone with a sound grasp of what is at stake.[10]

Remember, secularism is a jealous god, and it will have no other gods before it, which is why a proper understanding of theocracy is so important. Christians must understand something the Christians of the first three centuries of the church understood all too well: "Jesus Christ is Lord" is a political statement. If they refused to confess Caesar as Lord they were seen by the Roman state as a threat to its absolute power. This is exactly where we are in the twenty-first century West.

Boot further adds to our understanding of the faulty characterization of theocracy against those suggesting that a Puritan theocracy is about the coercive rule of men, or the church in the name of God, and therefore represents a terrifying fundamentalism threatening Western freedom, like Islamic *Sharia* and violent radicalism. Nothing could be further from the truth.[11]

In Boot's, *The Mission of God*, from which this quote is taken, to further clarify the distortion of theonomy and what it is not, he quotes Greg Bahnsen and Kenneth Gentry:

> Theonomic ethics does not call for every magistrate to institute the entirety of God's law. That would be a horrifying abuse of political authority, turning every sin (e.g., lust, laziness, discourtesy, coveting, back-biting, impatience) into civil crimes... [T]heonomic ethics holds that civil magistrates may enforce only those provisions of God's law which authorize penal sanctions against *narrowly defined kinds of outward misbehavior*. God's law sets an objective limit upon the magistrate beyond which he may not go, whereas other schools of thought have no way of arguing against the state growing into a "beast" that "lawlessly" claims every area of life as its jurisdiction (cf. 2 Thess. 2:3,7; Rev. 13:15-17)...

Boot continues clarifying the concept of theocracy/ theonomy:

> The contemporary Puritan view, then, does not hold that the magistrate must execute apostates and heretics. It does not propose to eliminate political pluralism for a monolithic form of government; neither

does it hold that democratic institutions and societies are contrary to biblical law. In fact the Puritan spirit is seen in the English Puritans who were champions of freedom, a free parliament and a free people, with king and country subject to God's law; a free people electing their own representative government. Theonomists therefore champion democratic procedures for the state, including free elections, open debate, and competing parties.[12]

Once we get rid of the distortion, then what makes a specific nation Christian is one ruled by the law of God under Christ. What it does *not* mean is being ruled by the church institute. Medieval Catholicism gave us that model, which was rejected in due course, as we saw, by the English from Alfred the Great, to Magna Carta, to the Glorious Revolution, and eventually to America's founding. But what would the rule of God's law in a society look like. To flesh that out in such a short space is impossible but having some idea will be helpful. My goal is to persuade Christians to simply be open to the concept of the law of God in Christ as the only Christian option against secular totalitarianism.

Before I address God's law proper, I want to establish the spiritual nature of this enterprise, of building a Christian nation. It can only come when a growing number of conservative Christians take the Great Commission and the dominion and cultural mandates seriously. It will be the work of the Holy Spirit (Zech. 4:6) as He applies Christ's redemption to His people. There are enough serious Bible believing Christians in American to make a fundamental difference, far more than the woke leftists who currently dominant politics and culture. The question is the will to do it, and the theological justification for it. There are also

a growing number of non-Christians, agnostics, and atheists who affirm Christianity as central to, and necessary
for, Western civilization to succeed. In other words, we
have allies who are not Christians in this existential war
against the totalitarian left, and this is deeply significant.
Part of the process, as I implied above, is educating non-
Christians that true liberty of conscience and freedom of
religion is *only* available in a Christian nation whose ultimate authority is the word and law of God, not the church
nor the state.

THE TWO TABLES OF THE LAW

This brings us to the Ten Commandments, often divided
into two tables, the first four addressing one's obligation
to worship God, and the last six one's civil obligations, the
vertical and horizontal if you will. Because of the influence
of secularism, it has become commonly accepted among
Christians and non-Christians that the state has no interest in legislating anything to do with the first table which
belongs to "religion." As we know from the infamous doctrine of the "separation of church and state," religion and
the state supposedly have nothing to do with one another,
which is manifestly untrue. The question is whose and what
religion will inform the state because morality comes from
religion, or faith in the ultimate meaning of things, and
what the people in a society accept as right and wrong. I've
argued for many years, there is no such thing as an unbeliever. All people live by faith and are religious. Therefore
what ultimately determines the laws of a nation is the religion of its people.

What is "controversial" and brings out cries of theocracy
or "Christian authoritarianism" is claiming the state should

recognize and formally acknowledge God in Christ. Until the latter half of the twentieth century, that nations could be Christian was commonly accepted and not in the least "controversial" in all Western societies of Christendom; previously indicated above regarding anti-blasphemy and Sabbath laws in America. The state has a role in promoting what people in the past called "true religion," which was Christianity. It is obvious today what "true religion" is, and the state is most definitely promoting it. I heard someone recently say the holy trinity of the modern secular world is reason, science, and technology; all good things that become idols for destruction when people absolutize them as if they could exist without God. Herbert Schlossberg tells us how intimately connected the two tables are, that you can't have the second without the first:

> Nobody who rejects the first four commandments' call to reject idols and worship the true and living God can be expected to recognize any ultimate significance in the last six commandments' ethical requirements.[13]

Look at the chaos in the so-called blue cities in America, secular havens all. Crime and lawlessness are rampant, families decimated, homeless people everywhere, portraying a tragic picture of what happens when God's law is abandoned, the antithesis of the liberty and flourishing that result when God's law is obeyed.

Today many Christians are in some way antinomians, meaning anti-law, as if the gospel and the law are mutually exclusive. In this view, with the advent of Christ and the gospel, the law of God revealed to His people Israel under the Old Covenant is no longer applicable in the New Covenant Age, but this is completely unbiblical. The state is established by God and should be acknowledged as its only legitimate source of authority and laws. The Christian base of the society must be acknowledged, then we can prudentially work out the details from there in any number of forms of government, including representative democracy. There is nothing total-itarian or tyrannical about it. It is also incorrect to make the modern nation-state analogous to Israel. Many Christians accuse we who believe God's law revealed in Scripture should be the basis of civil society of exactly that, as if we're trying to reinstitute Israel and all the details of its law and governance in America. That is a straw man and no person who embraces theonomy rightly considered believes it.

THE NECESSITY OF SPHERE SOVEREIGNTY

The concept of sphere sovereignty is critical in the nev-er-ending battle against the spirit of Babel. The concept is as simple as it is contested by those who embrace that spirit. It was first introduced by the great Dutch theologian, statesman, and journalist Abraham Kuyper (1837-1920) in a public address at the inauguration of the Free University of Amsterdam. The question comes down to authority and who wields it. Absolute sovereign authority rests in God alone, and He has delegated His authority on earth to human beings:

> so that on earth one actually does not meet God Himself in things visible, but that sovereign author-ity is always exercised through an office held by men.

In this he asks two pertinent questions:

> And in that assigning of God's Sovereignty to an office held by man the extremely important question arises:

how does that delegation of authority work? Is that all embracing Sovereignty of God delegated undivided to one single man; or does an earthly Sovereign possess the power to compel obedience only in a limited circle; a circle bordered by other circles in which another is Sovereign?

These spheres interact and overlap in society, but one sphere must never usurp the authority of the other. The only way this possibly works, and thus the only possibility of true liberty in any society, is the acknowledgement of the absolute Sovereignty of Christ. Kuyper explains why:

> But behold now the glorious Freedom idea! That perfect and absolute Sovereignty of the sinless Messiah at the same time contains the direct denial and challenge of all absolute Sovereignty on earth in sinful man; because of the division of life into spheres, each with its own Sovereignty.[14]

Stephen Wolfe explains it well:

> [I]t follows that every sphere of life requires a suitable authority, with a suitable power, to make determinations. For this reason, God has granted specific types of power by which the authorities of each sphere make judgments. The family has the pater familiar with patria potestas ("fatherly power"); civil life has the civil magistrate with civil power; the instituted church has the minister with spiritual power, and the individual has a power unto himself. The nature of each sphere dictates the species of power required. These powers and

their differences are not arbitrary but arise from the nature of each sphere.[15]

Although as a Thomist he attributes this to "natural law,"[16] there is nothing natural about it. It is only when those in power acknowledge the power of God in Christ as the ultimate authority that the state will recognize its limits.

Finally, in this context I must briefly mention Martin Luther and his world changing declaration at the Diet (assembly) of Worms in April 1521. He was commanded to appear to respond to charges of heresy in his writings, but Luther refused to repudiate his works unless convinced of error by Scripture or reason. Otherwise, he stated, his conscience was bound by the Word of God. The Holy Roman Emperor Charles V issued the Edict of Worms, a decree which condemned Luther as "a notorious heretic" and banned citizens of the Empire from propagating his ideas. Because of the Internet of the time, the printing press, this proved impossible and the idea of freedom of conscience was unleashed on the Western world.

It would lead to the concept of religious freedom when it was finally acknowledged what had been apparent as far back as ancient Israel. The state has no authority to compel anyone to believe anything against their will. The religion of Israel was never imposed on the foreigner or alien. Jesus is a wonderful example of this because He went out of His way to discourage people from following or believing in Him; it was their choice. Christians prior to Luther should have known better, and many did, but when the church got mixed in with the state, both became tyrannical. The individual in his thinking and actions has his own sphere of sovereignty within the confines of the law. While there were glimpses of this in English history, as in Oliver Cromwell's Protectorate, it wasn't until the Puritan-inspired first Great Awakening, and the American experiment in self-government coming in its wake, that true religious liberty was codified in the law of a nation, and to that Christian nation we turn next.

CHAPTER 12

THE FOUNDING OF AMERICA

In July of 2020, on my sixtieth birthday, my family gave me a framed print of Arnold Friberg's painting, "The Prayer at Valley Forge," which depicts George Washington kneeling in the snow at Valley Forge next to his great white stallion. Friberg was commissioned to do the painting for the Bicentennial of the Declaration of Independence in 1976. I had no idea at the time how important that print would become to me. You'll remember the summer of 2020. We were several months into "two weeks to flatten the curve," which would turn into two years of the Covid nightmare of worldwide government overreach and tyranny, the likes of which the world had never experienced. I had my eyes opened to the depth and breadth not only of the corruption of American government, but of the entire globalist cabal that was trying to build a tower of Babel right before our very eyes. Those running American government and culture were all in.

Considering all that had been happening since Trump came down the escalator, that print hanging in my office took on a whole new meaning. Although I knew it, I realized afresh the impossible odds of the American Revolution succeeding against the greatest military power on earth. The David and Goliath story has nothing on the American colonies against the mighty British Empire, which is why they prayed and implored God to come to their aid. Nobody expected the colonists to win. It was impossible, ridiculous, but God had other plans. In Patrick K. O'Donnell's *The Indispensables* we read a common sentiment of the time.

> "The madmen of Marblehead are preparing for an early campaign against his Majesty's troops," scoffed a Loyalist newspaper earlier in 1774, skeptical of the idea that Americans could threaten the most experienced and skillful military professionals on the planet at the time.[1]

He quotes a patriot later in the year, "The idea of taking up arms against Great Britain is shocking but if we must become slaves or fly to Arms I shall not hesitate one moment . . ."[2] In *Washington's Immortals*, O'Donnell states:

> most of the world at the time believed it ludicrous to suppose that a ragtag assortment of amateurs with their unique set of principles could stand up to—let alone defeat—one of the finest armies in existence."[3]

Myles Cooper, the president of King's College in New York and a dedicated loyalist, said what most Americans was afraid was true: "To Believe America able to withstand England is a dreadful infatuation."[4] Many thought it foolish, a waste of blood and treasure that would no doubt prove futile.

Not long after the signing of the Declaration of Independence the Revolution looked to be over before it had even started. That summer of 1776 the British were intent on ending this pesky threat to their sovereign rule over their colonies and crush the rebellion. The British government sent a large fleet along with more than 34,000 troops to New York. In August, the British forces under General William Howe routed the Continental Army on Long Island surrounding them on all sides with the East River to their back and giving them no possible means of winning the battle. Instead of surrendering, Washington decided to evacuate the army and retreat to Manhattan, a decision that saved the Continental Army and the patriot cause. Providentially, on the night of August 29, a storm blew in from the northeast preventing the British from sailing up the East River which allowed Washington the time to order every flat bottom boat and sloop in Manhattan and the Bronx be sent to Brooklyn. Washington watched as 9,000 men were silently smuggled across the East River to Manhattan, and as the sun came up, a fog miraculously descended on the remaining men crossing the river. According to eyewitnesses, Washington was the last man to leave Brooklyn, gliding away on the last boat having saved his army and the future nation.

After the escapes, the fall and early winter would prove the lowest point in the war for American independence. Casualties and desertions growing day by day, Washington and the Continental Army were pushed to the breaking point. In November, while traveling with the army, the author of the wildly popular *Common Sense*, Thomas Paine, penned his famous *The American Crisis* that emboldened the demoralized army:

> THESE are the times that try men's souls. The summer soldier and the sunshine patriot will, in this crisis, shrink from the service of their country; but he that stands by it now, deserves the love and thanks

of man and woman. Tyranny, like hell, is not easily conquered; yet we have this consolation with
us, that the harder the conflict, the more glorious
the triumph. What we obtain too cheap, we esteem
too lightly: it is dearness only that gives everything
its value. Heaven knows how to put a proper price
upon its goods; and it would be strange indeed if
so celestial an article as FREEDOM should not be
highly rated.

Paine's words ignited anew the fires of independence, and
while there were to be many more difficult days and nights
ahead, the hope of victory could never be extinguished. The
following year at Valley Forge was brutal, the army enduring starvation and illness. The story of Washington praying
alone in the woods at yet another bleak time, a la Friberg's
painting, is supposedly legendary, but Washington knew as
did other American leaders, that without God's help they
had no chance.

When I look at the painting every morning and pray
for America to survive the current crisis, I see our time as
analogous to America's founding. The odds of us defeating
America's current enemies are great, but I've realized the
odds against those first American patriots were far greater.
Our enemies seek to establish a global empire and want, in
Obama's words, to fundamentally transform America as
founded. We will not let them.

As modern American patriots can attest, these too "are
the times that try men's souls," and this too is no time
for "the summer soldier and sunshine patriot." We see
such an attitude of defeat among those given to gloom-
and-doom, what I call "doomers." They believe things are
so bad that America as we know it is over. I beg to differ,

strongly. I am convinced, as are many, God in His providence, mercy, and grace, used the Covid nightmare among many other travesties to create another Great Awakening. In the immortal words of another heroic Patriot, we "have not yet begun to fight." This was Captain John Paul Jones' fearless reply when he was charged to surrender as he and his crew engaged in a desperate battle with a British frigate off the northern coast of England in 1779. To know why we should fight, we must first understand how the dynamics of providence in history allowed America to be founded, and how those same dynamics can help in re-founding it today. To reiterate what Paul said, in God's providence as Christians and Americans, this is our "appointed time" (Acts 17:26). The call to extend Christ's reign, advance God's kingdom, and build his church is as pressing in our day as it was in Paul's.

PERSPECTIVES ON AMERICA'S FOUNDING

Not only are we in an existential battle for the soul of our country, but we are also in a battle for defining how America was founded, what it meant then, and what it means in our present historical moment. There may be as many different perspectives as there are multitudes of books written on the subject, even among Christians and conservatives. I will outline three broad perspectives driven by the worldview of the people who hold them. Christians believe, like the Founders, America was providentially founded—a God-ordained reality from beginning to end. The other two we encounter in this battle are secular liberalism and cultural Marxist leftism. I paint with extremely broad-brush strokes because having a handle on these other views is necessary if we're to defeat them.

CULTURAL MARXIST LEFTISM

We'll start with the latter and its most egregious distortion, a perversion really, coming from the left-wing "newspaper of record," *The New York Times 1619 Project*. Most Americans are probably like me, they've heard of it, but knowing it's Marxist claptrap they've never bothered to read anything about it. When you ingest some of this distasteful mess, you'll realize just how distorted it is, as in funhouse mirror distortion. Jake Silverstein wrote the introduction, and he comments on the claim that slavery is:

> sometimes referred to the country's original sin, but it is more than that: It is the country's very origin. Out of slavery—and the anti-black racism it required—grew nearly everything that has truly made America exceptional: it's economic might, its industrial power, its electoral system, its diet and popular music, the inequities of its public health and education, its astonishing penchant for violence, its income inequality, the example it sets for the world as a land of freedom and equality, its slang, its legal system and the endemic racial fears and hatreds that continue to plague it to this day. The seeds of all that were planted long before our official birth date, in 1776, when men known as our founders formally declared independence form Britian.[5]

Other than that, America's great! Although absurd on the face of it, the cultural Marxists control much of American culture and government and believe it to their core. They push it on a public in an attempt to indoctrinate them for their perpetual Marxist revolution.

When I went to college ('78- '82), such anti-American hatred was common, primarily in the social sciences, but it was Howard Zinn's best-selling 1980 book, *A People's History*, when we see Marxist American history begin to make its way into public education. Unlike the inscrutable writings of American-hating academics, *A People's History* is cultural Marxism for dummies in the guise of history. Timothy Goeglein writes:

> Zinn singlehandedly transformed the study of history in American public education from the discipline of surveying facts and events to the displaying of "reframing" and "reimagining" facts to fit a particular narrative.[6]

This narrative is perfectly consistent with *The 1619 Project*. It may surprise us how few Americans believe this narrative, given our monolithic left-wing culture. I've marveled at this for decades because such indoctrination is nothing new, only today it's more overt. Over the years whenever I would go to Fourth of July celebrations I would look around at the multitudes of people and think, no way they hate America like the lefties do. My conclusion? The American spirit cannot be snuffed out by the left, so thankfully we have something to work with as we rebuild our country.

SECULAR LIBERALISM

I've already laid my cards on the table regarding the myth of neutrality. Secularism and liberalism both lead inevitably to where we are now, toward Babel and away from liberty. To the secular liberal, the seventeenth- and eighteenth-century Enlightenment was the primary *secular* influence on America's Founders. That is demonstrably untrue. Mark David Hall in *Did America Have a Christian Founding?* dismantles that contention, but shows even respected Christian historians like Mark Noll, Nathan Hatch, and George Marsden claim America's Founders were primarily Deists and Unitarians and "not in any traditional sense Christian."[7] As I argued previously, none of America's most famous founders were doctrinaire Deists, and the rest were in fact orthodox Christians. Hall contends only one, Ethan Allen, could be considered such a Deist.

This is not to say, however, that the Enlightenment did not influence the Founders, but as we also saw previously, there were various tributaries of Enlightenment thinking. It is clear from the results of the American and French Revolutions the two embraced very different Enlightenment influences, the latter embracing secularist, rationalist, and anti-Christian ideas, while the former a held to a rationalism based on Scripture, Christianity, and traditional American culture. The French revolutionaries rejected everything coming before. They worshipped the Goddess of Reason, and the results were anarchy, bloodshed, and eventually the tyranny of Napoleon. The American Revolution could not have been any different, from its influences to its results: true liberty, and the separation of powers against the spirit of Babel.

Some people claim the inspiration of America's founding is something called classical liberalism. For many years, since modern conservatism seemed to be on quite a losing streak, I figured maybe I was a classical liberal. I'm all for liberty, after all, hate big government and the tyranny it brings. However, I started to sour on the term when I realized many who embraced it were libertarian in all but name. For them, liberty was the highest good, and I realized it just can't be. My freedom and liberty have to come from somewhere and can't stand alone as any kind of ultimate moral good. America's Founders understood this. There's a long history behind classical liberalism, including profound Christian influences, but that's far outside the scope of this book. What I can say is what I've already said, secularism in any guise, including liberalism, will always and everywhere eventually return to Babel.

I want to emphasize that any modern liberalism should be rejected by Christians aware of mankind's penchant for Babel. As for classical liberalism, some Christians and con-servatives think a classical liberalism is possible apart from the God of Scripture revealed ultimately in Christ. It is not! They don't believe secular neutrality is a myth but think it's necessary for a vital, pluralistic public square where all voices can be heard and respected. How's that working out for us so far? If you bring up Christianity and specifically Christ as the sole sovereign over all government authority (Eph. 1:20, 21) to which presidents and kings and prime ministers must submit, cries of theocracy ring out, and off to the Spanish Inquisition we go. I hope I adequately laid that fear to rest, and we'll see that outside of the context of Christianity, the American experiment could have never happened, nor can it endure.

Unfortunately, many conservatives fall into classical lib-eralism's trap thinking they can have their secular cake and eat it too. This is the "natural law" trap, as if laws could ultimately be rooted in anything other than revelation in creation, Scripture, and Christ—it's a package deal. Laws, morals, right and wrong *must* come from somewhere, and the appeal *must* be to some higher authority than matter, i.e., nature. So my first question when I see that phrase is, where does "natural law" come from? Natural law *must* have a law giver, and the Founders knew it came from the God of the Bible, full stop. To the "founders" of the French Revolution, it came from nothing more than "mere reason," and the horrific results were inevitable.

Edward J. Erler writes about an inter-conservative squabble between Harry Jaffa and Willmoore Kendall and their progeny, one going on since conservative was a thing not long after World War II. This paragraph makes clear Erler falls into the trap:

> What was its attraction for Kendall? It was pre-Locke—although that didn't preclude it having "Lockean" elements—it didn't mention equality, and it did, albeit in passing, make a bow to Christianity, whereas the Declaration's "Laws of Nature and of Nature's God" seemed to make a secular reference to Divine Providence. Kendall mistakenly interpreted the language of the Mayflower Compact to have created a Christian people for America and this became a part of the American political tradition. The version of Divine Providence that appears in the Declaration was an appeal to all sects within Christianity as well as all religions.[8]

This could not be more wrong nor more futile as the foundation for a lasting and flourishing republic as the Founders well knew. The further America has gotten away from Christianity, the further away it has gotten from liberty. It is Christianity alone that provides the only true, lasting foundation for liberty. It's clear you can't have one without the other, and abstract "rights" built on "natural law" will never get the job done. Whatever liberalism is and its actual influence on America's Founders, it could only develop into true liberty and limited government (i.e., against Babel) as it did in the context of a country founded by Christians that would turn into a thoroughly Protestant Bible drenched nation by God's providence.

CHRISTIANITY AND THE DEVELOPMENT OF THE AMERICAN CONSCIOUSNESS

To hear some tell it, America of the later eighteenth century was an Enlightenment paradise filled with French philosophes. Even Jefferson who might come closest to that description was at first excited about the French Revolution, but soon became disillusioned by the brutality and bloodshed. He could even be mistaken for a Christian at times in his public pronouncements, whatever he personally believed. Just as human beings don't grow up in a vacuum, neither do nations; we all come from somewhere, as did America. The influences are innumerable, but the Christian contours are easy to trace, for those without a secular ax to grind.

English settlement started in North America with Jamestown and Captain John Smith, but the origins of the American consciousness really began with the great Puritan migration to New England from the 1620s through the early 1640s. We all know the story of the Mayflower which arrived in November 1620 to establish Plymouth, the first colony in New England. Under the leadership of William Bradford, 102 Puritans known as Pilgrims, separatists escaping religious persecution in England, sailed for North America. The famous Mayflower Compact was a document signed on the ship prior to its landing at Plymouth, Massachusetts, and was the first framework of government written and enacted in what became the United States of America. Self-government is in the genes of those who came to America, and not just the Puritans.

The 1630s migration was led by another Puritan leader, John Winthrop, who settled Massachusetts Bay Colony, modern Boston, in June 1630. Winthrop, like Bradford and all Puritans, believed the God of the Hebrews and their Savior was a covenant making God who promised faithfulness and blessing if they remained committed to obedience and His glory. As he penned the famous words, if they were faithful "we shall be as a City upon a Hill. The eyes of all people are upon us." And if not, they "shall be made a story and byword through the world."[9] Winthrop's conviction that the success of this experiment depended on the blessing of obedience to God is also in the American genes. I will quote but one example, a few lines from the first inaugural address of George Washington:

> Such being the impressions under which I have, in obedience to the public summons, repaired to the present station; it would be peculiarly improper to omit in this first official Act, my fervent supplications to that Almighty Being who rules over the Universe, who presides in the Councils of Nations, and whose providential aids can supply every human defect, that his benediction may consecrate to the liberties and happiness of the People of the United States... Every step, by which they have advanced to the character of an independent nation, seems to have been distinguished by some token of providential agency... And in the important revolution just accomplished... cannot be compared with the means by which most Governments have been established, without some return of pious gratitude along with an humble anticipation of the future blessings which the past seem to presage.

Washington is basically echoing the spirit of Winthrop. Various studies have shown the Bible is the most quoted book of the Founders and the founding generation, Deuteronomy being one of the favorites, especially Chapter 28 of the blessings for obedience and curses for disobedience.

But it wasn't just Puritans and New England. America wouldn't have become America if its development had not happened exactly the way it did with a variety of British peoples moving so far from home confronting the daunting American geography, a situation unique in the history of the world. If there is a history textbook that should replace Howard Zinn's Marxist inversion of the truth, it's *A Patriot's History of the United States* by Larry Schweikart and Michael Allen. They masterfully tell the story of how these circumstances are without parallel in history, how a new world was forming a people whose character, mentality, and vision was forged for liberty and self-government in an unforgiving land of boundless opportunity far from their motherland. I would love to explore some of these fascinating details, but space won't allow it.

The First Great Awakening of the 1730s and 40s was another powerful influence on the social and political life of Americans for it drove the implications of Christianity deep into the American consciousness. Given this move of God's Spirit was antiauthoritarian and democratic, the Crown would not have been happy about it. Robert Curry agrees, saying "the Great Awakening prepared the way for the American Revolution in too many ways to be counted."[10] Pulpits across America, influential in a way modern Americans can't comprehend, were aflame with justifications for liberty and revolution. Americans as Englishmen saw their rights earned centuries before being blithely discarded by the British government. None of this was in the realm of abstract "rights" intellectual conservatives love to argue about. It was real, boots on the ground, everyday living as self-governing people before God who granted them the liberty to live their own lives. Americans were eminently practical people, including its intellectual leaders. Russel Kirk shows how the founding was not some abstract intellectual debate about "natural rights":

> When educated Americans of that century approved a writer, commonly it was because his books confirmed well their American experience, justified their American institutions, appealed to convictions they had held already: with few exceptions, the Americans were not fond of intellectual novelties.[11]

That sounds absolutely right to me. Yoram Hazony confirms this, commenting on Kirk about Anglo-American constitutionalism not being deduced from influential seventeenth century philosopher John Locke but emerging from "a century and a half of civil social order in North America and more than seven centuries of British experience."[12]

And, I would add, without the specific Protestant versions of Christianity they all embraced to one degree or another, none of this happens. Here is a quotation from *A Patriot's History* to emphasize the ubiquity of Christianity in the American consciousness of the eighteenth century. Writing about something every colonial settler and western pioneer understood:

> [C]haracter was tied to a Christian tradition, which was then tied to liberty through a widespread acceptance of common law, and liberty to property—preserved and protected by titles and deeds and, soon,

by a free market. All four were needed for success, but character was the prerequisite because it put the law behind property agreements, and it set responsibility right next to liberty. And the surest way to ensure the presence of good character was to keep God at the center of one's life, community, and ultimately, nation... It went back to that link between liberty and responsibility, and no one could be taken seriously who was not responsible to God. "Where the Spirit of the Lord is, there is liberty." They believed those words.[13]

All of America's Founders and the founding generation believed this. The quote on the Liberty Bell from Leviticus 25:10 reflects this, "Proclaim liberty throughout the land to all its inhabitants." The Founders clearly didn't see a contradiction between liberty and the Bible or Christianity. There wasn't a secularist in the lot of them!

A COMMONSENSE NATION

America's intellectual class was as dialed in to Enlightenment ideas as anybody could be at the time, but the ideas coming from Europe would take on a distinctly American cast through the influence of scholars and clergy who brought ideas of the Scottish Enlightenment to colonial America. These ideas combined with the unique circumstances and the Founders' genius allowed them to create something entirely new in the history of the world. The primary influence of the Scottish thinking on the Americans was Thomas Reid and what came to be called Scottish common sense realism. This philosophy was a pushback against two philosophical streams at the time. The first was a rationalism that eventually led to the skepticism of the also Scottish David Hume, that basically knowledge is impossible. The second was the subjective idealism of George Berkely, the idea that nothing exists except minds and spirits and their perceptions or ideas. People, especially Americans, were hungry for the real, and common-sense realism gave it to them. The idea is simple. Common sense realism states we all have innate ideas that can be known and don't have to be taught to us. As esoteric as this may all sound, it had world transforming implications for the America of the late eighteenth century and its politics, grounding human knowing not in isolated human reason, but in moral sense.

This is important for the debate over the Declaration and what it means that,

> We hold these truths to be self-evident, that all men are created equal, that they are endowed by their Creator with certain unalienable Rights, that among these are Life, Liberty and the pursuit of Happiness.

Was this primarily a secular reference to things divine as Mr. Erler above claims, or something deeper? Is this something solely grounded in reason universally applicable to all people in all places and times, or something deeper, rooted in time and place and circumstance? Well, yes. Our version of democracy didn't work in the Middle East, for example, because there was no Christianity, or the development of the rule of law and limited powers. These things develop slowly over time and can't be imposed as if they only have to be rationally understood to be implemented. They aren't so "self-evident" after all, but they can be grasped by common people given the right circumstances and worldview—a biblical worldview.

Common sense philosophy was also important for establishing the most unique idea of the founding argued initially by Locke but rooted in something deeper by the Founders—popular sovereignty. In societies previously, only the ruling elite were seen as capable of ruling the common people. That all radically changed in America as stated by Robert Curry:

> Here then is the rock upon which the Founders will build their idea of republican self-government: because a person who is capable of acting with common prudence in the conduct of life is capable of discovering what is true and what is false in matters that are self-evident, self-government is possible.[14]

This is quite the contrast to Plato's *Republic* and his argument for the necessity of a philosopher king. In America, every man could be his own philosopher king having the common sense to govern himself and his family, and sovereignly run his only little piece of society himself. The Founders also differed from Locke, who made the protection of property the fundamental purpose of government, but property is alienable, it can be given up. The Founders on the other hand made our rights unalienable because we could never give up life, liberty, and our pursuit of happiness, nor could they be taken from us, not at least without a fight. Curry adds to the rock upon which the Founders will build their idea of limited government:

> [Because] the rightful purpose of government is securing its citizens' unalienable rights, government is necessarily limited government, limited because its reach is defined by the vast field of liberty reserved for the citizens.[15]

Vast field of liberty, I like that! The Founders could make such arguments because of the Hebrew and Christian idea of a personal Creator God of Scripture and man made in His image everywhere assumed and taught in American culture of the time; not to mention the Christian England and common law tradition bequeathed to the Founders since Alfred the Great, and these ideas developing over centuries. No wonder the Marxists and secular globalist elites hate Christianity and do everything in their power to enervate and destroy it!

Before I leave the Scot's influence on America's founding, I must mention something I only learned as I was researching for the book; as a Presbyterian I was most gratified to learn of it. It isn't just philosophy where the Scots' influenced the founding, but in the development of how people thought of government. According to Curry:

> John Knox, the Martin Luther of the Scottish Reformation, founded the Presbyterian Church in 1560-1561. Long before the Founders began to make their argument for popular sovereignty, Knox preached popular sovereignty as a matter of doctrine. Political authority, Knox taught and the Presbyterians believed, ultimately belonged to the people. According to Knox, the people had the right to choose those who would manage their political affairs, and it was the people's right to remove them at will.[16]

The church, or as the Scottish called it, the Kirk, from the beginning was a representative system of government, unheard of in the world up to that time. The entire way the Kirk was managed was representative from top to bottom. Curry adds:

Both the doctrine of popular sovereignty and a functioning representative governing body that embodied the doctrine of popular sovereignty were unique to Scotland during the time.[17]

Knox also laid the theological foundations for the right of Christians to resist wicked rulers. Most Christians at the time believed it was morally wrong to revolt against the king. In fact, many people during the revolution called it a Presbyterian revolution.

The Puritans, Presbyterians, and Congregationalists who then came to America brought these ideas with them and they eventually made their way into the consciousness of Americans. Douglas Kelly says it well:

Over the next six or seven generations, these Calvinist-based ideas would be worked out in various church and civil polity experiments and then would be combined with a variety of other (in the later period, secular) theories of government and liberty to give rise to the movement leading to the American War of Independence and to shape its constitutional settlement.[18]

To claim Christianity and liberty are somehow at odds is contrary to historical facts, not to mention the theological truths revealed to us in Scripture.

However, it wasn't just the Presbyterians who had an impact on the shape of the American government, it was also the variety of types of British peoples who came to carve out new lives in the vast wilderness of America. They all brought Protestant Christian convictions with them, including how their churches and communities should be governed. These convictions permeated the colonies and in due course influenced the ideas of the Founders. It's worth sharing two quotes from Mark A. Beliles and Stephen K. McDowell as they make this critical point:

> Even as none of the forms of church government alone constitutes the biblical model, so also the Christian form of civil government must be a composite of all three. Episcopalian, Presbyterian and Congregational forms *together* make biblical church government. Monarchy, aristocracy and democracy *together* makes a biblical civil republic. This is indeed what God providentially arranged in the establishment of the United States of America.[19]

Providentially indeed! The second quote is longer and for me deepens the marvelously providential nature of America's founding:

> Just as federalism was an idea rooted in church government, so also is the concept of the three branches of government. The Protestant Reformation produced three distinct movements of Christians who emphasized three different forms of church government. The Episcopalians emphasized the rule of one from the top down. The Presbyterians emphasized the rule of a few elders. Congregationalists emphasized the rule of many. By the design of Providence, each of these groups colonized America and formed their colonial governments in patterns similar to their churches. The northern colonies, settled predominantly by Congregationalists, established a form of democracy. The Sothern colonies, being mostly Episcopalian,

established "Royal Provinces" which were a form of monarchy. The middle colonies were proprietary, and being influence greatly by Reformed Presbyterianism established more aristocratic governments.[20]

Again, remember what I said above. We're in a battle to define how America was founded, what it meant then and what it means now. Of all people, Christians need to know America as founded was the fruit of a thoroughly Christian tree, as all the historical facts attest, and we only scratched the barest of surfaces here. If we are to return to America as founded, whatever that might look like in the twenty-first century, it is to these facts that we must cling, for without Christianity and Christians deeply involved, there will be no re-founding. To the hope of that we turn next.

CHAPTER 13

THE RE-FOUNDING OF AMERICA

I must say, bluntly, whose fault it is that the United States of America as founded has been lost, destroyed almost beyond recognition by its Marxist enemies: *you and me*! That's right, it's *our* fault. In the last several years as I've encountered doomers, both personally and online, I have always been frustrated by their defeatism and negativity. I recoil from this victim mentality and from those without hope who don't believe they have agency, that they can change things, and who believe there are powers and forces beyond their control who determine their lives. This is not a mentality worthy of Christians or Americans, least of all Christian Americans. If America's Founding generation saw reality this way there would be no America and none of us would exist. Thank God they didn't. And neither should we.

The beauty and the danger of the American experiment in republican self-government is that its success or failure depends on us. Benjamin Franklin said it best. Upon leaving the Constitutional Convention a woman asked him what kind of government we had. "A republic, if you can keep it," was his response. Franklin, the supposed Deist, also understood upon whom the success of this experiment ultimately depended. At the convention where the details of this experiment were being hashed out, he said these words to the august attendees which could come out of the mouth of any fervent Evangelical of that time or now:

> I have lived, Sir, a long time, and the longer I live, the more convincing proofs I see of this truth, that God governs in the affairs of men. And if a sparrow cannot fall to the ground without His notice, is it probable that an empire can rise without His aid? We have been assured, Sir, in the Sacred Writings, that "except the Lord build the House, they labor in vain that build it." I firmly believe this; and I also believe that without His concurring aid we shall succeed in this political building no better than the Builders of Babel.

He couldn't say it any better for the theme of this book, and for all those today who war against the ever-present threat of Babel in our time.

As we saw, America is a self-governing republic where the people are sovereign, but the genius of the Founders not only affirmed rule with consent of the governed, but also checks and balances in government. The French thinker Montesquieu was a primary inspiration for that, but it was the dominant Calvinistic Protestantism of the day that gave them the theological and anthropological categories to conceive it. Calvinism teaches the doctrine of total depravity, not that every person is as sinful as they can be, but that every aspect of man is infected by sin. Thus, we can't be trusted with absolute power, and the genius of the American Constitution as written. This didn't apply only to those in office, but to the masses as well. Being keen observers of history, the Founders knew the people could abuse their corporate power because they too are sinners, but the substantive power of "We the people" was real and something never before given to a people in the history of the world. We just don't take advantage of it.

I must quote from an article written in *The Atlantic* in April 1877 by the twentieth president of the United States, James A. Garfield, then a member of the US House of Representatives. It is called "A Century of Congress," and he reflects on the history of American government focusing on Congress and its importance to a well-functioning republic. It could not be timelier nor more apropos for our day because of the inherent fragility of this experiment of government of, by, and for the people (in Lincoln's memorable phrase):

> [N]ow, more than ever before, the people are responsible for the character of their Congress. If that body be ignorant, reckless, and corrupt, it is because the people tolerate ignorance, recklessness, and corruption. If it be intelligent, brave, and pure, it is because the people demand those high qualities to represent them in the national legislature... The most alarming feature of our situation is the fact that so many citizens of high character and solid judgment pay but little attention to the sources of political power, to the selection of those who shall make their laws. The clergy, the faculties of colleges, and many of the leading business men of the community never attend the township caucus, the city primaries, or the county convention; but they allow the less intelligent and the more selfish and corrupt members of the community to make the slates and "run the machine" of politics. They wait until the machine has done its work, and then, in surprise and horror at the ignorance and corruption in public office, sigh for the return of that mythical period called the "better and purer days of

the republic." It is precisely this neglect of the first steps in our political processes that has made possible the worst evils of our system.

Chalk this up to the more things change... I like the way someone in our day, Eric Metaxas, states the opportunity and danger inherent in the American system of government:

> [B]y itself the Constitution could do very little. What it promised would require the efforts of all those who henceforth called themselves Americans. It was they who must keep it, the republic and the grand and noble promise of that republic. That is the wonderful, spectacular genius of it all, and the terrible, sobering danger of it all too. The document and the men who created it put these unimaginably great and fragile things in the hands of the people.[1]

Here's the deal. We have no one to blame but ourselves. The finger pointers, and I've been among them, have given up their agency, their God-given ability to change things. As I taught my kids growing up, taking responsibility *is* freedom. It gives us hope that we're not mere pinballs at the mercy of the great Pinball Wizard in the sky, cogs in the proverbial wheel that cares not how much sand we put in the gears. Such a victim mindset would have been completely foreign to the founding generation, and it needs to become foreign to us as well, not just in our personal lives as important as that is, but in our corporate lives as American citizens. General Washington said in 1777:

> We should never despair, our Situation before has been unpromising and has changed for the better,

so I trust, it will again. If new difficulties arise, we must only put forth new exertions and proportion our efforts to the exigency of the times.[2]

He could not imagine the exigencies of our time, but he would certainly implore us to new exertions. Ronald Reagan, that great President of liberty, did implore us with these eloquent words:

> Freedom is never more than one generation away from extinction. We didn't pass it to our children in the bloodstream. It must be fought for, protected, and handed on for them to do the same, or one day we will spend our sunset years telling our children and our children's children what it was once like in the United States where men were free.[3]

As I often say, we are fighting against the fall. Everything naturally goes downhill. Any dead fish can float downstream. The second law of thermodynamics applies to societies, to cultures, and governments. From the liberty granted to us in 1776 to our government formed in 1787, these *must* be fought for and if necessary, in the words of Churchill, "with blood, toil, tears and sweat," protected, and handed to generations to come. No more whining and belly aching; let's get on with it!

"WE THE PEOPLE OF THE UNITED STATES, IN ORDER TO FORM A MORE PERFECT UNION... "

You will recognize these as some of the most famous words in the English language, and certainly among the most momentous. They are the first words in our Constitution and have changed the world in too many ways to count.

The fifty-five men who wrote and signed the Constitution all agreed with George Washington, the most respected and revered member of the convention, when he wrote:

> If, to please the people, we offer what we ourselves disapprove, how can we afterwards defend our work? Let us raise a standard to which the wise and honest can repair. The event is in the hand of God.[4]

I bring up God yet again, because most importantly we must understand that we are not in this alone as all the Founders believed. We've been given promises from God we can count on if we would but live by faith and not sight. Each one of us must get to a point where we either believe God wants us to win, or not. We must believe God wants to bless us, and that we live in a cause-and-effect universe where sowing brings reaping—that what we have been given in this the greatest experiment in human government is worth fighting for. I could quote verses all day that meld God's sovereign power with human responsibility. As I've heard it put, work like it depends on you, but pray because it depends on God. However I will limit myself to a few before we explore some details of how we might fight for America.

The first is from King David's battle with the formidable Ammonites in 2 Samuel 10. Joab the commander of David's army spoke to the troops prior to battle:

> [12] Be strong, and let us fight bravely for our people and the cities of our God. The Lord will do what is good in his sight."

We trust God with what we can do and leave the results to Him. These words from 2 Chronicles 7, familiar to many

Christians, reveal our God who is never deaf to the pleas of His people:

> ¹⁴ if my people, who are called by my name, will humble themselves and pray and seek my face and turn from their wicked ways, then I will hear from heaven, and I will forgive their sin and will heal their land.

Although spoken by the Lord at the dedication of Solomon's temple, this is not just for the people or nation of Israel. Christians in every nation of the world are His people, and God can heal every land.

The next passage comes after the glory of Israel has been decimated by civil war and foreign conquest. There is still a remnant left in Judah, including the prophet Jeremiah who writes a letter to the exiles in Babylon (Chapter 29). False prophets have given the exiles false hope their troubles will be over soon, and they'll be headed back to Judea in no time, but that is not to be the case. He commands them to plan for the long term:

> ⁴ This is what the Lord Almighty, the God of Israel, says to all those I carried into exile from Jerusalem to Babylon: ⁵ "Build houses and settle down; plant gardens and eat what they produce. ⁶ Marry and have sons and daughters; find wives for your sons and give your daughters in marriage, so that they too may have sons and daughters. Increase in number there; do not decrease. ⁷ Also, seek the peace and prosperity of the city to which I have carried you into exile. Pray to the Lord for it, because if it prospers, you too will prosper."

In one way we are all always and everywhere exiles in a *fallen* world, but this is God's world, and He has placed us in our time to fulfill the dominion mandate under King Jesus and take it back. As we do and pray, and pray and do, we too can prosper. And finally, we go decades later when the exiles have come back to Jerusalem and are trying to rebuild their city amidst opposition and obstacles. Nehemiah (Chapter 4) is trying to encourage the people:

> [14] After I looked things over, I stood up and said to the nobles, the officials and the rest of the people, "Don't be afraid of them. Remember the Lord, who is great and awesome, and fight for your families, your sons and your daughters, your wives and your homes."

And he adds: "Our God will fight for us!" It is these for which we fight, and for those yet to be born.

Now what? Before we discuss a few ideas, I want you to notice the somewhat humble ambitions of America's Founders. They were under no illusions they could form a perfect union. Breathing in the sweet Calvinist air of the time, they aspired to "a more perfect Union." It was to this end they established a republican form of government outlined in the Constitution. The challenge and the work will always remain because in this fallen world it will never be perfect, thus we must remain ever vigilant and not do what so many of us have done over the decades—take it for granted.

THE WONDERS OF FEDERALISM

In June 2017, after having lived in Illinois for seventeen years we escaped to Florida. I was dumbfounded by the number of out-of-state license plates; I'd never seen anything like it. I was told it was "snowbirds" from the north. In June? I was also told by friends and family it was people moving from "blue" states who would bring their voting habits with them and turn Florida blue. I didn't think so. I believed most of these people were refugees like us, looking for something of the liberty America promises to its citizens. The distinction between the two states became more apparent after the Covid saga, although for too long Florida bought into the panic as well. In 2017 Florida was almost a purple state with over 350,000 more registered Democrats than Republicans. The increasing number of out-of-state license plates continues to this day and still amazes me. As of December 31, 2023, there were 779,701 more registered Republicans! That is federalism, and the genius of the Founders still working 247 years later.

This doesn't happen anywhere else in the world. Americans are leaving blue states like California, New York, and Illinois for red states in droves because those states are run differently. So, for those moaning about America as founded being gone, enough remains from which to rebuild. I don't know details of how other Western countries run their governments, but in Canada, for example, people couldn't move from one province to another to avoid the Covid vaccine mandates. In fact, we had a family move to Tampa and attend our church for a year because the father was unwilling to get the vaccine. They had to leave their country! We don't. The point is that as bad as things appear, as big and out of control as Leviathan (the federal government) has gotten, federalism is not dead. There is still a great measure of sovereignty in the states to run things as they see fit.

What is federalism and why is it so wonderful? Since we're looking to re-found America, it is important to have a clear idea of what America looked like *as* founded. In the previous chapter we focused more on the religious and philosophical underpinnings for the inspiration of America's founding, and to one degree or another we need to get back to that to have a chance to accomplish our mission. That's one side of the war, the broader cultural side, the why. The other side is the narrower question of how we maximize liberty in the context of the actual details of how government, both federal and state, operate. Always keeping the spirit of Babel in mind, we'll look at the true enemy we face, but it is helpful to see how the founding generation dealt with the same dynamic; Babel never sleeps. We can see this dynamic and what we're up against in the differences between what were known at the time as the Federalists and the Antifederalists.

The Federalists wanted a stronger national government, and the Antifederalists wanted a weaker national government with stronger state governments. Now I'm praising federalism because I want a weaker national government and stronger state governments. Stick with me.

The Federalists were instrumental in shaping the Constitution, which strengthened the national government at the expense, according to the Antifederalists, of the states and the people. The Antifederalists opposed the ratification of the Constitution, but they never organized effectively across all thirteen states, and it was eventually passed. They did, however, force the first Congress under the new Constitution to establish a bill of rights to ensure liberties the Antifederalists felt the Constitution violated. They also forced the Federalists, like James Madison, to emphasize the necessity of the federal government having limited power as he does in *Federalist 45*:

> The powers delegated by the proposed Constitution to the federal government are few and defined. Those

which are to remain in the State governments are numerous and indefinite.

And thus, the tenth amendment to the Constitution:

The powers not delegated to the United States by the Constitution, nor prohibited by it to the States, are reserved to the States respectively, or to the people.

Many of us are familiar with the saying, the government that governs least, governs best, but that's not quite right. It's more accurate to say a government that governs according to well-defined limits is the government that governs best.

The reason a constitution was necessary was because previously under the Articles of Confederation the United States government wasn't working. A weak federal government and 13 completely independent sovereign states was proving to be a disaster. Under such an arrangement the union would be difficult if not impossible to maintain, thus the calling of a Constitutional Convention in 1787. Needless to say, their efforts have been a monumental success, but it is clear now the fears of the Antifederalists were well-founded; we are living with the consequences. Leviathan needs to be cut down to size, and the modern sense of Federalism needs to be rebuilt.

THE GROWTH OF THE ADMINISTRATIVE STATE AND THE FAILURE OF CONSERVATISM

Like most Americans until the last handful of years, I hadn't even heard the phrase administrative state, also referred to as the deep state or the swamp; some accurately calling it the fourth branch of government. Simply, it's the unelected bureaucracy running the country, which Trump is vowing to dismantle if he's elected president again in November 2024. That is one reason he is so reviled and hated among the nation's ruling class—he's learned lessons from his first term and since. The dismal circumstances in which we find ourselves have been over a hundred years in the making, and it's taken many of us a long time to realize we are in a war for the soul of the American experiment as a republic, a representative democracy ruled by "We the people." To put it in the starkest terms possible, it is Babel verses anti-Babel, and there is no in-between. There is no compromising with Babel; you may as well compromise with Satan himself.

Philip Hamburger, the foremost scholar and critic of the administrative state calls it extralegal, meaning it is inherently antithetical to the rule of law. As we saw in the English development of the common law tradition over the last thousand plus years, this battle of rulers against law is nothing new. He explains why:

> Administrative power is extralegal, or outside the law, in the sense that it attempts to bind Americans not through law, but through other mechanisms. The traditional common law ideal, secured in the Constitution, is that government can bind its subjects only through the law—meaning only through legislative acts and acts of the courts of law. In contrast, in the absolutist traditions of the civil law, the government can bind subjects through other, prerogative or administrative edicts. This is not government through law, but extralegal power that runs outside the law.[5]

Without the rule of law, all we have is the will to power, or those who have the power impose their will. The fundamental problem is the lack of accountability as he further explains:

> Administrative power leaves ordinary Americans . . . with no opportunity to vote for or against their administrative lawmakers. Unelected bureaucrats can impose policies without concern about being voted out of office. Unsurprisingly, they feel less accountable than elected legislators to . . . ordinary Americans.
>
> This isolation of policymakers from politics was, of course, one of the reasons for establishing the administrative state. It is often said that the goal was to protect experts from political pressure, but from the outset, an underlying aim was to cut ordinary Americans out of key decision-making.[6]

Hamburger argues that Woodrow Wilson is the "founding father of the American administrative state." As an academic, Wilson wrote a paper in 1887 arguing for "the science of administration," which speaks to the rule by "experts." This rule by "experts" became the rage in the progressive era of the early twentieth century. In the last hundred-plus years we've witnessed the kudzu-like growth of the administrative state, not realizing that like the plant it is a "rampant invasive species" that quickly spreads over trees and shrubs (republican government), often killing them. Our elected representatives have turned over much of their legislative power to unelected bureaucrats so they don't have to be accountable to the people they represent. They see it as job protection, thinking whatever the results are it won't get them fired. This is done primarily through federal agencies initially created by congress giving unelected bureaucrats the power to create regulations that have the force of law without congressional oversight.

Which brings me to the futility of the conservative movement; what I now call Con Inc. As conservatives we always wonder why no matter what party wins elections, nothing seems to change—government just gets bigger and more intrusive in our lives. Most conservatives and Republicans are no better than the controlled opposition. They've completely accepted the progressive gains of the last hundred years, and their assumptions, merely pushing for slower and less, which always leads to more of the same. It's proved a lucrative grift for those without principles. I've known for a while, well before Trump, that something was wrong, but I could never clearly identify what it was. Why is our side so adept at losing? Prior to the 2016 election, Michael Anton in his famous "The Flight 93 Election," nailed it:

> If you're among the subspecies of conservative intellectual or politician, you've accepted—perhaps not consciously, but unmistakably—your status on the roster of the Washington Generals of American politics. Your job is to show up and lose, but you are a necessary part of the show and you do get paid. To the extent that you are ever on the winning side of anything, it's as sophists who help the Davoisie oligarchy rationalize open borders, lower wages, outsourcing, de-industrialization, trade giveaways, and endless, pointless, winless war.

Not to mention ignoring the destruction of America as founded by the administrative state.

The failure of the conservative movement was baked into the cake of conservatism when in 1951 its ostensible founder, William F. Buckley, Jr., released his first book, *God and Man at Yale*. He accepted the principal assumptions of liberalism, what R.R. Reno calls the "open society" of the "post-war consensus." In *Return of the Strong Gods*, Reno argues that conservatism and libertarianism, two sides of the same coin, embraced the assumptions of post-war liberalism with its hostility, or at least indifference, to metaphysics and the transcendent. Reno highlights the thinking of sociologist Max Weber from his famous address "Science as a Vocation" (1917) inspiring what developed as a completely secular "consensus":

> Weber presented disenchantment as a hard fate. Modern man has no choice but to put aside religious claims and with them the old, metaphysical worldviews of the West. We must navigate through life by the cold light of scientific reason and govern societies in accord with empirical analysis of observable phenomena.[7]

What Reno calls the "scientific reconstruction of society," Weber would term "disenchantment," and would change from being a "hard fate," something unpalatable, to being redemptive to post World War II Elites. Commenting on Karl Popper's *Open Society and Its Enemies* he states:

> The Postwar consensus embraces "critical thinking" as an indispensable cultural therapy, necessary to

prevent the development of the authoritarian personality and forestall the return of totalitarianism.[8]

Prior to reading Reno's book, I knew libertarianism was
in effect a reaction against nineteenth century totalitarianism and collectivism, and in some sense determined by
it. I didn't realize, though, how much conservatism was as
well. Thankfully, and the reason for this book, we are witnessing what Reno calls the dying of the postwar consensus.
Therein lies our opportunity but it won't happen without
you and me.

CIVIC ENGAGEMENT IN A SELF-GOVERNING REPUBLIC

This is not the place to explore in detail what civic engagement will look like for each person given that's not the
purpose of this book. It will look different for each one of us
depending on our talents, aspirations, age, commitments,
resources, etc. As the Apostle Paul said, different parts of
the body have different functions, but they are all of value
and necessary.

For most of my life I've seen the key to changing our
country happening from the top down. I was wrong. Many
Americans agree with me, realizing nobody is coming to
the rescue, that if our country is to be saved it is going
to be up to us—we the people. Change must happen in
large part from the bottom up, at the local level. We've
become fat, happy, and lazy believing if we just vote things
will take care of themselves. That is no longer an option.
Clearly, they won't. This is a challenge for those of us of
a conservative bent who, like me, just want to live our
lives, take care of our families, and enjoy God's blessings.
I know the 80/20 rule is a fact of life, that twenty percent

of the people do eighty percent of the work and vice versa, but desperate times call for desperate measures. We must encourage each other to get involved or lose the right to complain. But what if twenty percent of God-fearing patriotic Americans actually got involved? We could turn the world upside down!

Those inclined to run for public office can serve in local city government, or county, or even at the state level. This is a heavy commitment which is why we need to pray for God to raise up Godly men and women of integrity committed to America's founding principles. Those not so inclined must hold accountable those who are. This takes time and often money. It means showing up, writing e-mails, and making calls. I started seeing the possibilities of this when I discovered Steve Bannon's *War Room*. There are patriots all over the country who realize the desperate times in which we live, and Bannon offered me a window to see this happening. It's one of the reasons after the 2020 election and J6 fiascos I turned from a pessimist into an optimist. Because of the genius of the Founding Fathers, even as far gone as America now is, there are still many legal, peaceful means to fight back and defeat America's enemies.

One thing my wife and I have done which doesn't require an extensive commitment is become precinct committeemen in our local county GOP. On *War Room* in February of 2021, I learned about something called the Precinct Strategy on his show as a means for conservatives to take over the Republican Party. There are over 400,000 of these positions throughout the country, and at least half are empty. This is a travesty. We could take over the Republican Party through the Precinct Strategy if only a fraction of the conservatives who complain about how bad things are got involved. We can become voting members of the Party and make the RINOs who are not committed to America as founded extinct. If I've pricked your conscience at all, go to precinctstrategy.com and learn how.

Unlike the Democrat Party, the Republican Party was developed to be run from the ground up to truly reflect what America is as a self-governing representative republic. People can be involved a little or a lot or anywhere in between, but I've seen this make a difference at the ground level in various states. I always think about those 200,000 empty positions when I see people complain.

MY PRAYER FOR OUR COUNTRY

I write this as an American living in America, but what I'm saying applies to Christians in every nation. The command of Jesus in the Great Commission (Matt. 28) was to "all nations, baptizing them in the name of the Father and of the Son and of the Holy Spirit, and teaching them to obey everything" he commanded them. God in his providence has allowed the ideas of the rule of law, liberty, and representative democracy that came to fruition in America's founding to spread throughout the world, so Christians in "all nations" can apply the same blessings in the unique situations and cultures in which they live.

When I pray for our country, I pray for revival, restoration, renewal, and reformation because America has no chance of recovering its founding principles in a secular nation. Francis Schaeffer in his 1981 book, *A Christian Manifesto*, writes of the idea of antithesis, or two opposite diametrically opposed forces, in our case worldviews; it is either biblical Christianity or secularism—there is no in between. Schaeffer argued a shift was taking place *from* something at least vaguely Christian:

toward something completely different—toward a worldview based upon the idea that the final reality is impersonal matter or energy shaped into its present form by impersonal chance... These two worldviews stand as totals in complete antithesis to each other in content and also in their natural results... not only in how they understand the nature of reality and existence. They also inevitably produce totally different results. The operative word here is *inevitably.* It is not just that they happen to bring forth different results, but it is absolutely *inevitable* that they will bring forth different results.[9]

Now in 2024 we are living with the full flowering of those inevitable results. If I were a betting man I would wager a lot of money that there were many well-meaning Christians in the early 1980s who said Schaeffer was being hyperbolic and paranoid. He wasn't. History bears him out—he was being prophetic. I remember many asking at the time why he was getting so "political." Because he knew there is no neutrality, and the alternative to Christianity is, as I've called it, the new paganism, secularism.

I pray the four R's because most Christians don't understand the antithesis. They think revival is about "saving souls" and making us more moral people, which indeed it is, but it is so much more. It is applying the Christian worldview to all of life, extending Christ's reign over every square inch of life, advancing His kingdom, and building His church. Ours is a *gospel* mission. The Founders affirmed repeatedly that without a virtuous people who were capable of self-government, a constitution was merely ink on paper. As John Adams wrote in one of the most well-known of these affirmations:

> Our Constitution was made only for a moral and reli-
> gious people. It is wholly inadequate for the govern-
> ment of any other.

And by a religious people he meant a Christian people.

The self-understanding of Americans until the late 1800s, and as I've argued really until post–World War II, was that we were indeed a Christian nation. In 1892 the United States Supreme court affirmed something unimaginable to Americans today in a case providentially titled, *Church of the Holy Trinity v. The United States*, that America "is a Christian nation."

And for those who still think Christian means narrow and intolerant, a Christian nation must and will appeal to all Americans, not just Christian Americans, because it works! It creates peace and harmony by creating stable families, establishes and defends the rule of law where the scales of justice actually balance, promotes the liberty of our persons and minds that our Christian founding granted us, and promises the blessing of prosperity of a people who live according to the Ten Commandments. Yes, this won't happen overnight, as neither did the dismantling we've witnessed over the last one hundred years, but gradual change is change nonetheless, and that starts with you and me.

As I pray those four R's, I'm usually looking at the print of Washington in "The Prayer at Valley Forge." In the plaque below the print is a statement Washington made in December 1773, when he resigned as Commander in Chief of the Continental Army and retired to his home at Mount Vernon, Virginia. In words similar to what he would repeat in his two terms as president, he said:

> I consider it an indispensable duty to close this last
> solemn act of my Official life, by commending the

Interests of our dearest Country to the protection of Almighty God, and those who have the superintendence of them, to his holy keeping.

Amen, and Amen.

ESCHATOLOGY: THE THEOLOGICAL FOUNDATION FOR OPTIMISM

This final chapter, fittingly, is about eschatology, the study of last things, specifically, how history will end. I'm excited to write it because postmillennialism, which is the subject, is little known among Evangelicals, most thinking it's a completely discredited position as I did until last year when it completely blindsided me. I am confident those who feel this way know as much about it as I did, which is absolutely nothing, and that might be exaggerating the extent of my knowledge. I *thought* I knew what postmillennialism was and rejected it as even worthy of consideration. I've learned this is true for most Christians, even the most well read and knowledgeable Christians. Regardless of whether you agree with me or not, when you get to the end, at least you will know more than I ever did. What I soon realized was the more I learned, the more I discovered how properly understanding postmillennialism provided the framework for everything I'd been thinking regarding the theme of this book. Of necessity, this will be a cursory examination, but I hope it's enough to establish the theological justification for my optimism.

MY ESCHATOLOGICAL JOURNEY

Much of this book is my story, and when I started the very last thing I thought it would include was embracing postmillennialism. When I was born-again in the fall of 1978, officially becoming a Protestant Christian (I grew up Catholic), dispensational premillennialism was ubiquitous. That's hard to imagine now because the topic is all but invisible, even though most Christians are dispensational premillennialists (whether they can articulate it or not). The basic idea is that before Jesus returns world events the Bible supposedly predicts will get really ugly. Then comes the rapture when true Christians will be taken out of the world to escape the suffering of a seven-year tribulation—horrific judgment of God on earth—then Jesus will return to reign on earth for a thousand years, or something like that. This was the default Evangelical position, the "end-times" air we breathed. Hal Lindsey's *The Late Great Planet Earth* was one of the best-selling books of the 1970s and discussion of these things was everywhere. Over time the endless speculation, what some call newspaper eschatology, got tiring and I quit paying attention.

When I went to seminary in 1986, I was exposed to the other two prominent positions, amillennialism and post-millennialism, but I don't remember being much interested in the topic, probably because I was burned out by the hype of the dispensational take on premillennialism. Over time I turned into a "pan-millennialist" because trying to understand "end times" made eschatology seem like endless speculation and trying to figure it all out was a fool's errand. I was an agnostic; I figured it would all pan out in the end. I concluded we can't really *know* anything about eschatology with any certainty so why bother. Then in 2014 I discovered amillennialism and learned maybe there actually was a biblical eschatology, meaning one based on exegesis, gaining our understanding out of the text of Scripture, instead of speculation. For the next eight years the word postmillennialism never entered my mind until the summer of 2022, August to be exact.

My journey to postmillennialism and the reasons I rejected it are similar to others who've "converted" to it later in life, especially those of us who grew up in the 70s, 80s, and 90s. I rejected it because of what we discussed previously, nineteenth and early twentieth century cultural conditioning of the Western concept of "progress." The hubris coming out of Enlightenment rationalism and the explosion of scientific knowledge led people to assume progress was linear, like an arrow shot directly to ever more wonderful human accomplishment. I thought Christians at the time uncritically conflated this secular idea of progress as their eschatology, including my theological heroes, the great Princeton theologians Charles Hodge and B.B. Warfield. Apparently, they were great in all things theological, except when it came to eschatology.

As I started thinking about and writing this book in early 2022, I realized I needed theological justification for my optimism, especially given I had never been optimistic about anything related to culture or politics. As conservatives in the later part of the twentieth century we knew we were the underdogs. I've mentioned how Steve Bannon and his War Room got me out of my funk after the 2020 election, and somehow listening to him almost daily turned me into an optimist even though he's a gritty realist who pulls no punches. He preaches agency, meaning that it isn't hopeless for America after all, that as patriots, conservatives,

Christians, we can actually change things. But I was sensing it was something much deeper than that.

Being amillennial I had no ready theological category for optimism.[1] I was thinking I might find my justification in the revelation of God in creation a la Paul in Romans 1:20, that "God's invisible qualities—his eternal power and divine nature—have been clearly seen, being understood from what has been made... " In other words, because of God's revelation in creation, and human knowledge is part of His creation, we now know things we wouldn't have known before Trump, or before Einstein, or before America's Founding Fathers, or before Aquinas, Luther, Locke; you get the picture. The sum of all human knowledge is in some way a revelation of God's "eternal power and divine nature." I thought this was a promising avenue until postmillennialism dropped out of the sky on my head. God's revelation in creation is still part of the answer, but only because now I have the theological categories in the eschatology of postmillennialism.

But I hadn't put two and two together until I heard Doug Wilson say, "Now you have a theological justification for optimism." That's it! That moment of realization was electric. I found what I was looking for in a place I didn't even know existed.

Before I give a brief overview of postmillennialism, I will give an even briefer overview of the alternatives for those new to the topic.

PREMILLENNIALISM AND AMILLENNIALISM AND THE PENCHANT FOR DOOM

The three broad positions have in common a word meaning a thousand, millennium, and comes from one chapter near the end of the Bible, Revelation 20, the reference to Satan being bound for a thousand years. Those who adopt the pre-position believe Christ will return to earth *before* the millennium and reign a literal thousand years while Satan is bound. Both the other positions believe the thousand years is not literal and indicates approximately the time from Christ's resurrection and ascension to His return or second coming in which Satan is bound while Christ builds His church and advances His kingdom. The latter is where the two part ways as we'll explore below. As I implied above, premillennialism has two versions, dispensational and historical. The former is the new kid on the block having been invented, if you will, in the mid-nineteenth century. The rapture and dispensations (different distinct time periods of God's working in history) distinguish the two versions of premillennialism.

That's as much as I will say because there is plenty of material available for anyone interested in learning more. My objective here is to explain why I reject these and now believe postmillennialism is the biblical position.

All Christians believe Christ will return to judge the living and the dead, and will reign forever with His people on a restored earth. We all agree on the most important thing, that Christ will return and reign, so to make eschatology a point of contention is unnecessary. We also all believe the Great Commission is meant to bring the gospel throughout the earth to peoples of all languages and cultures and build Christ's church. What separates us is the implication of the gospel and the Great Commission for this fallen world prior to Christ's return. Speaking of postmillennialism David Bahnsen captures the essential point:

> The cause of an optimistic eschatology has never been one of enlightening one's view of the future as much as informing their activity in the present.[2]

In other words, eschatology is more about the present which we can know and experience than the future which we can't. Yes, we all know the end of the story. The question is how the end affects the now and in what ways.

Prior to my recent "conversion," starting when I discovered Bannon, I was a doomer given to pessimism, as if Christians were destined to cultural and societal defeat. I once heard John MacArthur, a staunch premillennialist, say, "Down here we lose, up there we win." Even if I might not have put it so starkly, I basically believed we lose down here, as do most Christians because there are so few postmillennialists. As I understood the cosmic drama played out on earth, things will inevitably get increasingly worse until Jesus returns, and like in the old 1960s campy Batman series, Bang! Pow! Wham! He saves the day! All the bad guys get put down, and Jesus sets things right in an instant. I tended to believe this because like many Christians I thought this world belonged to Satan. After all, Paul calls him the god of this age or world (2 Cor. 4:4), and Jesus refers to him as the prince or ruler of this world (John 12:31; 16:11). It is an understandable perspective given all the evil, suffering, and misery we see every day. Unfortunately, many Christians underestimate the power of God and overestimate the power of the devil, as if he was a formidable foe practically on equal footing with God. Once after something especially horrific happened a friend said, "This is Satan's world." Prior to my "conversion" I would have probably agreed. Now, I thought, No it's not! I replied, "Yeah, like a puppet on a string." In fact, as Paul says in that passage, the devil is the god of those "who are perishing" not the world God created "very good" in which we live.

Speaking of the perishing world, when I was young, ambitious, and naïve I believed I could "change the world."

As I got older and grew more jaded by my obvious inability to do so, I mocked my younger self for thinking something so preposterous. My younger self was right! I *can* change the world! In fact, we all can, and are called to do just that! That's the point of God so loving the world "that he gave his one and only Son, that whoever believes in him shall not perish but have eternal life." I almost saw salvation primarily as fire insurance so we can go to heaven when we die, according to N.T. Wright a profoundly unbiblical position, and I now agree with him.[3] I thought salvation was primarily for saving the souls of individual people, and the real, substantive transformation of the world would have to wait until Christ returns and makes all things right. I came across a perfect example of how I used to think from the magazine of my alma mater, Westminster Seminary. The issue is about global missions, and in one of the articles the author states what he sees as the mission of the church of Jesus Christ: "God is calling people to Himself out of every nation... "[4] Prior to my "conversion" I wouldn't have given this a second thought, but now my response was, "No, He's calling us to disciple the nations to see them transformed by the gospel!"

There are a significant number of Evangelical leaders in America who think Christian cultural influence is nice and all, but that it's a distraction from the important work of the church. I heard a sermon on regeneration typifying this mentality. The pastor said, "Those focusing on the culture wars are rearranging the deck chairs on the Titanic." Before my "conversion" this would have still bothered me because I've always believed Christians need to engage the culture at every level, but now with the theological framework of post-millennialism I completely reject such a view as unbiblical. Thankfully, after the last handful of years, many Evangelical leaders who embrace the pre-mill position are fully engaged in the "culture wars." After all, Francis Schaeffer was an historical premillennialist and he's inspired generations of Christians to be fully engaged in culture. In my experience most Christians who embrace premillennialism, whether they are more or less knowledgeable about it, long to see the culture and the world Christianized, but their theological framework won't allow them to believe such a thing can be achieved. To that we turn next.

WHY POSTMILLENNIALISM

What is postmillennialism? I think the title of an N.T. Wright book captures it well: *Jesus and the Victory of God*. Wright doesn't consider himself a postmillennialist, but he does understand that the victory of God in Christ has ramifications for this fallen world, of bringing heaven to earth. He calls it "inaugurated eschatology." Who doesn't like victory? Who doesn't want to be on the winning side? Being a third generation Dodger's fan, I was over the moon when they won the World Series in 1988. Initially it appeared they didn't have a chance against the mighty Oakland A's, not until the utterly improbable walk-off home run by the gimpy Kirk Gibson in the bottom of the ninth inning. That was only game one, but in a moment, we went from underdogs and certain losers to the inevitable winners. That's postmillennialism!

Christ commenced or inaugurated his kingdom on earth, but will only fully consummate it in the future, the already and the not yet applied to more than personal salvation. In other words, what Christ achieved in its ultimate consummated state in eternity is being realized in this fallen world gradually in time. As I've heard it said, God is a patient incrementalist, or as I often put it, God is *never* in a hurry.

Jesus tells us His victory, "Thy kingdom come, thy will be done on earth as it is in heaven," will happen slowly, waiting for water to boil slowly. How do we know this? He says as much in the parables of the mustard seed and the yeast in Matthew 13:31-33. His kingdom doesn't come to earth in a final, cataclysmic event as I used to believe, but slowly, gradually, often imperceptibly; without the eyes of faith at times it doesn't seem to be coming at all.

These parables tied it all together for me. Simply put Jesus' reign "on earth as it is in heaven" doesn't come all at once. It started when He fulfilled His mission on earth, redemption accomplished, and ascended to heaven to the right hand of God and sent the Holy Spirit at Pentecost, redemption applied. The mustard seed had been planted, and over time, a very long time, it will grow into the largest tree in the garden. The yeast or leaven is mixed into a very big batch of dough, and slowly influences every part of the dough. These parables completely changed my perspective on "end times." The question is, of course, what exactly all this looks like, and the Bible gives us plenty of answers.

My embrace of postmillennialism goes back a long way, although I didn't see it that way until now. When I was sixteen, my very Catholic grandmother gave me a novel called *The Robe*. It's the story of the Centurion who oversaw Jesus' crucifixion. John 19:23, 24 tell us the soldiers cast lots for Jesus' garment, and this Centurion won it. It seriously messed him up emotionally and psychologically, but eventually he embraced Christianity, and in his travels throughout the Judean countryside he brought peace and harmony and light everywhere he went. People got better and started to like and help one another instead of arguing and backbiting. I remember thinking at that young age I'd like to be that kind of person! Well, we *all* can be because the victory of God in

Christ is assured, and He sent His Holy Spirit at Pentecost to guarantee it. That in a nutshell is postmillennialism, Christ extending His reign throughout the earth, advancing His kingdom in our lives and sphere of influence, and being part of Him building His church. I realized we are Christ's body on earth, His eyes, ears, hands, arms, and legs. We represent Him bringing His kingdom influence to push back the fall and bring God's shalom to the four corners of the earth, starting at home. Paul tells us, "Christ always leads us in triumphal procession, and through us spreads the fragrance of the knowledge of him everywhere" (2 Cor. 2:14). Always. And the Greek word for triumph is beautiful—according to Strong's Concordance, to display triumph openly; publicly exalting the victor who leads a victory-procession – and putting the conquered on display (exhibition, as "totally defeated"). That's my kind of fragrance!

The beauty of Christianity is that it isn't just personally transformational but transformational in every way: societal, technological, relational, material, etc. It effects every single thing human beings put their minds and efforts to in the light of God's word, the gospel, and His law, for our good and His glory. These blessings will eventually leak out from God's people to bless society. And we are never under the illusion these blessings are *solely* due to us, but they can't happen without us. Jordan Peterson, one of the most important Christian apologists of the twenty-first century even though his Christianity isn't fully formed as we would understand it, sees Christianity as essential to bringing order out of the natural chaos of life. He's studied evil probably more than any person alive, and he sees Christianity as the answer. As Christians, we should oblige him by bringing our faith into every nook and cranny of life and "infect" the people around us with a positive vision for the future.

Lorraine Boettner puts the postmillennial perspective in its definitive terms:

> We hold that Christ is not merely the potential victor, but the actual victor over sin. During the interadventual reign He is steadily putting into effect the victory that He has won, gradually overcoming the forces of evil, until all His enemies shall have been made the footstool of His feet (Acts 2:35).[5]

He also speaks of purposefully using "the word 'conquest,' rather than 'conflict,' for Christ is not merely striving against evil, but progressively overcoming it."[6] We are all familiar with the passage from Matthew 16:18 when Jesus says He will build His church, "and the gates of hell will not overcome it." I never realized I was interpreting this incorrectly all my Christian life. I thought Satan and his minions and the evil they perpetuate were on the *offensive*, and it was Christians and the church who are on the *defensive*. That is exactly backward! Gates in the ancient world were *defensive* mechanisms. It is the church enabled by God the Holy Spirit that is on the *offensive*—Satan and his kingdom don't stand a chance!

I don't know about you, but I'm excited to be on the winning team!

THE BIBLICAL CASE FOR VICTORY

I will analyze some texts, but before I do I want to emphasize something critical to my argument. I used to automatically interpret the texts I will reference as applying to *the eternal consummated state* in the new heavens and earth. My eschatology required it. With my new eschatological glasses, I now see the victory passages taking place on *this* earth in *this* fallen world, here and now, and the most obvious meaning of the texts. First, I will discuss the implications of a critical biblical word, bless.

In a lecture overviewing Genesis,[7] Dr. Mark Futato of Reformed Theological Seminary argues the key text of the book comes from Chapter 12:

> The Lord had said to Abram, "Go from your country, your people and your father's household to the land I will show you.
> [2] "I will make you into a great nation,
>   and I will bless you;
> I will make your name great,
>   and you will be a blessing.
> [3] I will bless those who bless you,
>   and whoever curses you I will curse;
> and all peoples on earth
>   will be blessed through you."

The key theme from these verses is "blessing for the nations." God is specifically establishing His covenant with Abram so through him and his offspring the nations will be blessed. If Dr. Futato were to reduce Genesis to one word it would be blessing which is used over 65 times. What struck me was his definition of blessing: empowerment. When God blesses people He empowers them to do a wide variety of things, as he puts it, "God empowers people to flourish." I love that! Secularists paint Christianity as repressive and intolerant, but what it represses and doesn't tolerate is sin! Sin destroys everything it touches and makes true flourishing impossible. It is by definition dis-empowering. Jumping forward two thousand years, Jesus says the same thing (John 10:10):

> The thief comes only to steal and kill and destroy;
> I have come that they may have life, and have
> it abundantly.

From Genesis 3 on, God promised this blessing through the seed of the woman. Jesus, that seed, will bruise or strike the serpent's head, while the serpent will bruise or strike his heal. The serpent can do some damage, but according to God he has no chance—an injured head is far worse than an injured heel. I like the NIV's translation of this verse, the seed will crush the serpent's head, but I don't think it's warranted by the Hebrew. Whatever the translation, it doesn't sound ambiguous to me; it has the scent of victory. I've come to see God's promise in the garden as the microcosm of all of history, and Jesus' words reflect that. His resurrection overcomes Adam's sin in space and time, and fully at His return and the consummation of all things.

We see throughout Genesis and in God's covenant promises to the Patriarchs that these blessings are to touch so many people they literally can't be counted (sand of the seashore, stars in the sky, and dust of the earth). God is not miserly in spreading His blessings on earth, and because of His covenant promise immediately after the fall, we realize all of it is done in the face of a cosmic spiritual war to frustrate the devil's plans. This means it will *never* be easy and will be done in the face of constant adversity and opposition, but through which we can rejoice in the victory already won by our risen Lord.

Because of limited space I will only focus on a handful of passages that sealed the deal for me not long into the journey of learning about the victory of God in Christ for the salvation of His creation.

PSALM 2

This Psalm is blatantly Messianic, and the only question is whether it applies to His first or second advent. It declares the futility of the nations who conspire and plot *in vain* "against the Lord and against his anointed." Of the Lord's king who He has installed on Zion, on His holy mountain, who He has declared His son, He says, "I will make the nations your inheritance, the ends of the earth your possession. You will break them with a rod of iron, you will dash them to pieces like pottery." Sounds like victory to me. Still, the question of when persists.

PSALM 110

In another blatantly Messianic Psalm we see the time question answered definitively in the key word, "until." Yahweh says to David's Lord He will sit at Yahweh's right hand (the place of ultimate authority and power) *until* He makes His enemies a footstool for His feet. This and the second Psalm are evocative of complete and total victory. Note is it while His enemies still exist.

I CORINTHIANS 15:25

Then we jump to the New Testament and the passage of Paul's glorious declaration of the resurrection of the dead. Paul clearly says Christ "must reign until He has put all His enemies under His feet." This *process* of reigning and ruling will continue *until* the final enemy will be destroyed, death. That is the second advent when Christ returns to judge the living and the dead.

When I saw these two Psalms connected with the I Corinthians passage I was stunned. For all these years I had no idea Jesus' victory over sin and this sinful world was not for some time far off in the by and by, but for here, for now—until!

EPHESIANS 1:20-23

Then I read this Ephesians passage with a whole new appreciation for the ascension. Prior to my "conversion" I heard someone say as Evangelicals we all but ignore the ascension, that there are almost never sermons in Evangelical churches on this most important fact of the Christian message. I realized he was right. I started thinking I need to pay more attention to our declaration that Christ, after He was raised from the dead, ascended to the right hand of the power of God as Psalm 110 predicted. We rightly focus on the resurrection, but that is only the beginning of the story. Paul says of Christ that God "seated Him at His right hand in the heavenly realms, far above all rule and authority, power and dominion, and every name that is invoked, not only in the present age but also in the one to come." I noticed the age to come was almost an afterthought. For Paul of primary importance was "the present age." How had I missed that all these years?

DANIEL 2:31-45

In the interpretation of Nebuchadnezzar's dream, Daniel tells him the statue he saw represents four kingdoms. He then sees a stone cut out, "but not by human hands. It struck the statue on its feet of iron and clay and smashed them." And this stone "became a huge mountain and filled the whole earth." Daniel then answers the question of when the "until" begins:

> 44 "In the time of those kings, the God of heaven will set up a kingdom that will never be destroyed, nor will it be left to another people. It will crush all those kingdoms and bring them to an end, but it will itself endure forever."

I always missed that this crushing (shattering or breaking in pieces in Hebrew) started 2000 years ago, not when Christ returns. As Andrew Sandlin says, "The everlasting kingdom predicted by God through Daniel is not established at Christ's Second Advent, but at his First Advent."[8]

ISAIAH 65:17-25

I have to give one obvious example of how my response to eschatological passages always used to jump to Christ's Second Advent. I never once, not a single time before post-millennialism, thought these passages could be referring to life in this fallen, messy, dysfunctional world where evil often is triumphant. Now I know that is exactly what they are referring to, "Thy kingdom come... " This passage was especially "knee-jerk" for me because it talks of "a new heavens and a new earth." Clearly this can't be *this* heavens and earth, the one we live in now. The Lord even says, "The former things will not be remembered, nor will they come to mind." How could it not refer to after Christ returns? Then we read this:

> 20 "Never again will there be in it
> an infant who lives but a few days,
> or an old man who does not live out his years;

the one who dies at a hundred
  will be thought a mere child;
the one who fails to reach a hundred
  will be considered accursed.

Wait. You mean death will still be a present reality in this "new heavens and new earth"? It appears so. But automatically because of my eschatological bias I thought this *has* to be metaphorical. After all, in verse 25 he says, "The wolf and the lamb will feed together, and the lion will eat straw like the ox." How can that be? I have no idea! I don't know where reality ends and metaphor necessarily begins, but this is only one passage. As they say in apologetics, it is a cumulative case argument, and now wearing those glasses I literally see it everywhere.

THE GREAT COMMISSION

I wish I could continue, but I must exercise self-control, so I will end with a passage all Evangelical Christians take seriously, Matthew 28:18-20:

> [18] Then Jesus came to them and said, "All authority in heaven and on earth has been given to me. [19] Therefore go and make disciples of all nations, baptizing them in the name of the Father and of the Son and of the Holy Spirit, [20] and teaching them to obey everything I have commanded you. And surely I am with you always, to the very end of the age."

First, Jesus says *all* authority, not some but all, has been given to Him. This includes every spiritual power as we saw, and every temporal power, every single one, every single president and king and prime minister and parliament and congress and mayor and Senator and I could go on. I used to moan about things government did, but now I realize nothing governments do would happen unless Jesus allowed it or caused it. Because of His authority, *therefore*, we are to go make disciples of the nations.

None of us who believe in biblical inspiration think any word is there by accident, and that is why the word nations is so important. As we saw previously, nations are a critical concept in Scripture. The Greek word Matthew uses here is ethnos, a race, people, or nation. Strikingly he didn't use a comparable Greek word for individual. His command was not to make disciples of individual people, but entire nations! Of course, all of Scripture is directed to individuals, but the point is the implications of the gospel for corporate people known as nations. Even though I believed this in some sense all my Christian life, my eschatological framework wouldn't allow me to really believe it. Now I understand it's what He always intended.

Finally, we know this conquering by Jesus is not in a worldly way, by the will to power, violence and coercion, tyranny and force. Commenting on Revelation 19, Greg Bahnsen points out that although on the surface the battle won appears bloody, it is clearly symbolic language because Jesus uses a sword that comes out of His mouth. As he says, "Jesus, now proclaiming the word of God and riding upon a white horse, goes out and He defeats all opposition— Victory in Jesus! *This is the Great Commission being fulfilled!*"[9] Even though the language of revelation is largely symbolic, I would never have connected Jesus' victory with the Great Commission, but it clearly can't be anything else because He "must reign until He has put all His enemies under His feet." By the almighty and irresistible power of the Holy Spirit, the victory is gained by reason and logic and persuasion, wrapped in a bow of service and love proclaiming the living Word of God.

A CONCLUDING POST-SCRIPT

Yes, the pun is intended. Because the book is imbued with a positive postmillennial perspective on Scripture, history, the present, and the future, I imagine many Christians secretly are hoping we postmillennialists are right. I want to reiterate, however, that to make eschatology a point of contention is completely counterproductive. Given the Visigoths are breaking through the walls, Christians can ill afford bickering over theological niceties, as important as those are. While in the trenches, it almost doesn't matter what we believe as long as we agree on who the enemy is and have a semblance of agreement on what victory looks like. In America, as I've argued, victory is America as founded. For orthodox Christians our ultimate faith in Christ unites us, but we should also work with non-Christians, people from every worldview and faith who are committed to the battle to save America and Christian Western civilization.

Everyone will agree, left, right, or center that Christianity is no longer a formative influence in Western culture. Yet, Christians across the theological spectrum long for their faith to be a formative influence on the culture. If this were not true, why do we complain about it so much! If you read the last chapter, you will know what I think the theological framework is to help us make that happen. But regardless of what our eschatological position is, we must reject a solely pietistic personal faith and passionately apply Christianity to all of life, including culture and politics. Otherwise, there is no end in sight for the misery and suffering to come.

Pietism has been a disaster for Christian cultural influence. I'm not speaking of personal piety and devotion, but the seventeenth century German Lutheran movement that became part of modern evangelicalism, especially after the Second Great Awakening. The focus turned toward a kind of spiritualism tending to emotionalism and feeling, and away from doctrine and cultural engagement. The personal salvation of individuals from hell became the primary concern of the pietist, not the glory, justice, and kingdom rule of God. Unfortunately, the cultural effect of Pietism was the weakening of the church and the strengthening of the state— as the church retreats the state inevitably grows stronger. Pietistic Christianity was unable to counter the influence of the Enlightenment, thus secularism triumphed, just as Lutheranism was unable to deal with the rise of the Third Reich. The Enlightenment saw the state, not the kingdom of God, as the truly universal concept by which we organize our lives. The church was considered an area of private faith and became a peripheral institution.[1] Many Christians are waking up to the fact that Pietism is no longer an option in a secular pagan Western culture—it's paganism or Christ. As I heard Doug Wilson put it, it's either Christ or chaos.

One of my goals is to appeal to people of every religion and no religion at all. I want to reiterate that here because the secular religious fanatics continually paint Christianity as regressive and intolerant, a ruse for Christians to take power and smother any and all dissent. Can you say Salem Witch Trials? Or The Handmaiden's Tale? I laugh when leftists try to compare Christianity to such tyranny, but there is more than a little historical precedent to justify a plausible distortion. Our objective as Christians should be to explode the myth of tyranny. Non-Christians need to see what most Americans saw in Christianity until the 1960s, including our Founders, and that is Christianity is the requirement for true human flourishing, and liberty and justice for all. As I've argued extensively, Christians are sadly mistaken if they think some neutral secular public square is the answer. Unfortunately, too many still do. It is Caesar or Christ.

I've written about red pilling, but there is another reverse awakening happening called black pilling, a mindset characterized by extreme pessimism, cynicism, and futility. In Chapter 11, I used the phrase "information war." War in the twenty-first century is not like it's been for millennia, kinetic, with bombs, guns, missiles, and the like. That kind of warfare in most instances is passe. Today, the most powerful weapon in warfare is information, which is used to control and exploit a population. This war is primarily by globalists against nation-states, sovereign peoples who want to determine their own destiny. The current American government, along with its corrupt media propaganda arm, is at war with the American people.

The primary strategy of the globalist technocratic elite is psychological operations (PSYOP). This has always been part of warfare in one way or another but is primarily how it's done today. PSYOPs are "operations to convey selected information and indicators to audiences to influence their emotions, motives, and objective reasoning, and ultimately the behavior of governments, organizations, groups, and individuals." Kinetic warfare is bloody and messy and destroys what the military is seeking to control and exploit. Information war, on the other hand, keeps resources intact to be used and controlled. The objective is to turn people into docile "sheeple" easily controlled for their own good. It is effective and daunting which is why many swallow the black pill figuring, why bother, I can't do anything about it anyway. The goal of PSYOP is sheeple and cynics.

All Babel totalitarians of the past believed they could create their utopia on earth with force and violence. The great totalitarian blood baths of the twentieth century driven by the likes of Hitler, Stalin, Mao, Pol Pot and friends failed miserably, but the Babel totalitarians learned from their mistakes, as did the classical economic Marxists, thus the woke world we now inhabit. Thankfully, twenty-first century information war totalitarians will be no more successful than the twentieth century version, and with this book I hope to do my small part in getting this message out. Because of the awakening an increasing number of people are getting it, and hope and determination are replacing pessimism and resignation. As I've said, an empire built on lies cannot stand. Many people think the left is winning. While the left also thinks they are winning, lying to have people think you're winning isn't the same as winning. Actually, that's only extending the brittleness of their empire and making it easier to take down.

Finally, evil is fundamentally irrational, which is what we see in the left's constant overreach. Because they are Marxists, they can never stop. They can't help themselves, and their very success is the means of their demise. We can see this all over the place, but it's most apparent in the trans madness. Redefining marriage wasn't good enough; they had to find some other oppressed group to exploit for the perpetual revolution. That God is giving them the desires of their hearts reveals the lies and the evil. Even the most apolitical people realize something is very rotten in Denmark. The reason they can't get away with it is what I call the

Guttenberg Press of the twenty-first century, the Internet. The globalists can no more control the Internet than the Catholic church could control the Reformation. Look at the response to Oliver Anthony's anthem, "Rich Men North of Richmond." As I write, on YouTube alone it has almost 115 million views and two hundred thousand comments. It's a worldwide phenomenon among every type of people who are sick of the globalists trying to control them and, in the process, ruining their lives. The secular/woke/globalist narrative our media has built is breaking wide open, and the truth is spilling out all over the place.

If we're not to fall prey to hopium and unrealistic optimism on the one hand, and a pessimistic cynicism on the other, we must embrace the Stockdale Paradox. Admiral James Stockdale was a United States Navy vice admiral and aviator who was awarded the Medal of Honor in the Vietnam War, during which he was held captive for over seven years as a prisoner of war in the infamous "Hanoi Hilton." As the senior naval officer among the prisoners, he was tortured routinely; his suffering was unimaginable.

The concept developed from his experience is found in the book *Good to Great* by Jim Collins. The idea is that productive change begins when you confront the brutal facts of a situation. There must be an unwavering faith in the cause prevailing in the end, regardless of the difficulties, and at the same time, have the discipline to confront the most brutal facts of the current reality, whatever they might be.

I didn't address in detail how we might tackle the daunting task of re-founding America and make Christian Western civilization happen because many are already doing that. But as a Christian I am convinced without Christianity that isn't going to happen. I also believe just as the First Great Awakening had a profound impact on the founding of America, the current Great awakening will also have a profound impact on its re-founding. Whatever that entails, I look at it much like eating the proverbial elephant, one bite at a time. Most people see the elephant and think, no way! That's impossible! It's huge! I would get crushed! While other folks just start eating one bite at a time. In due course they're picking their teeth sitting next to a massive pile of bones, while the other people are still complaining it can't be done. That's how all great endeavors are accomplished. As Teddy Roosevelt said, "It is not the critic who counts; not the man who points out how the strong man stumbles, or where the doer of deeds could have done them better. The credit belongs to the man who is actually in the arena." Let's get on with it.

Sole Deo Gloria

NOTES

Introduction

1. Yoram Hazony, *Conservatism: A Rediscovery* (Washington, DC: Regnery Gateway, 2022), Introduction.

2. In my previous book, *Uninvented, How the Bible Could Not Be Made Up, and the Evidence that Proves* it, I argue that the utterly unexpected nature of Jesus in the Jewish context of his world makes it impossible for him to have been made up or invented.

Chapter 1: Red Pills and the Next Awakening

1. Devin Nunes, *Countdown to Socialism* (New York: Encounter Books, 2020), p. 26.

2. Lee Smith, *The Permanent Coup: How Enemies Foreign and Domestic Targeted the American President* (New York: Center Street, 2020), p. 106.

3. I learned of this paper from a piece in Americanthinker.com By John Dale Dunn, "A Window on the Orwellian Dystopia of America" (August 27, 2022).

4. *The Bodies Others: The New Authoritarians, COVID-19 and The War Against the Human* (Fort Lauderdale, FL: All Seasons Press, 2022), p. 290, 291. After reading her book, it is impossible to put a benign spin on the Covid response.

Chapter 2: The Dividing Line in Western Culture: The Truth

1. https://threadreaderapp.com/thread/1301910526994321408.html

2. C.S. Lewis, *God in the Dock* (Grand Rapids, MI: Eerdmans, 1970), p. 58. Italics in original.

3. Francis Schaeffer, *The God Who Is There* (Downers Grove, IL: InterVarsity Press, 1968), p.13, 14.

4. Richard Weaver, *Ideas Have Consequences* (Chicago, IL: University of Chicago Press, 1984), p. 3.

5. I took this idea from Benjamin Wiker in his book *Moral Darwinism: How We Became Hedonists*. I will quote from my book, *The Persuasive Christian Parent* where I address this:

The scientific revolution of the sixteenth and seventeenth centuries asserted that the universe is a "closed system" (i.e., God is unnecessary for nature to work). There may be a God "out there," as pretty much all scientists believed at the time, but in due course they all became de facto Epicurean materialists. Benjamin Wiker explains how certain conceptual steps that led to the conclusion of a "closed system" were completely arbitrary. Nothing was ever proved. Rather, "Newton's Definitions, as ingenious as they and the rest of his work are, are by fiat: he did not demonstrate empirically that every body is composed of inert matter; rather the assertion was the presupposition that allowed for the desired universality, and for the application of geometry to all motions." In other words, in order to make the math work, Newton needed a Deist God, like the watchmaker who makes the watch that operates without any interference from its maker. P. 107.

6. Douglas Groothuis, *Truth Decay: Defending Christianity Against the Challenges of Postmodernism* (Downers Grove, IL: InterVarsity Press, 2000), p. 37.

7. Walter Kauffmann, *Nietzsche: Philosopher, Psychologist, Antichrist* (Princeton, NJ: Princeton University Press, 1974), p. 97.

8. "Stopping truth at the border: banning Michael Savage from Britain," By Selwyn Duke, May 6, 2009 (https://archive.ph/3jHER#selection-139.0-179.11).

9. "Live Not By Lies," Essay by Alexander Solzhenitsyn, February 12, 1974.

10. Ronald W. Reagan, Address to Members of the British Parliament, June 8, 1982.

Chapter 3: A Theology of History and The Providence of God

1. C.S. Lewis, *God in the Dock* (Grand Rapids, MI: Eerdmans, 1970), p. 15, 16.

2. Thomas Cahill, *The Gifts of the Jews: How a Tribe of Desert Nomads Changed the Way Everyone Thinks and Feels* (New York: Anchor Books, 1998) p. 94.

3. Vern S. Poythress, *Redeeming our Thinking About History: A God-Centered Approach* (Wheaton, IL: Crossway, 2022), p. 88.

4. Frederick Copleston, S.J., *A History of Philosophy*, Book 3, Volume 7 (Garden City, NY: Images Books, 1962), p. 219.

5. Ibid., p. 225.

6. Kauffmann, Ibid., p. 98.

7. Quoted in, "A Royal Ruin: Pascal's Argument from Humanity to Christianity," by Douglas Groothuis. http://www.bethinking.org /christian-beliefs/a-royal-ruin

Chapter 4: The Founding Generation and America's Providential View of History

1. Henry F. May, *The Enlightenment in America* (New York: Oxford University Press, 1976), Introduction.

2. Ellis Sandoz, Editor, *Political Sermons of the American Founding Era: 1730-1805* (Indianapolis: Liberty Press, 1991), Foreword.

3. Charles Firth, *Oliver Cromwell and the Rise of the Puritans in England* (United Kingdom: Putnam's Sons, 1900), p. 109, 167.

4. Tom Holland, *Dominion: How the Christian Revolution Remade the World* (New York: Basic Books, 2019), p. 17.

Chapter 5: The Delusions of Secularism and our Modern Discontents

1. R.C. Sproul, John Gerstner, Arthur Lindsley, *Classical Apologetics: A Rational Defense of the Christian Faith and a Critique of Presuppositional Apologetics* (Grand Rapids, MI: Zondervon, 1984), p. 3.

2. Ibid., p. 9, 10.

3. C.S. Lewis, *Christian Reflections* (Grand Rapids, MI: Eerdmans, 1995), p. 33.

4. James K.A. Smith, *How (Not) to be Secular: Reading Charles Taylor* (Grand Rapids, MI: Eerdmans), p. 18, 19.

5. Ibid., p. 47. Italics in the original.

6. Christian Smith, *Soul Searching: The Religious and Spiritual Lives of American Teenagers, National Study of Youth and Religion* (Notre Dame, IN: University of Notre Dame, 2005), p. 162, 163.

7. Smith, Ibid., p. 28, 29.

8. Charles Taylor, *The Malaise of Modernity* (Concord, Ontario: House of Anasi Press Limited, 1991), p. 69.

9. Alisdair MacIntyre, *After Virtue*, Second Edition (Notre Dame, IN: University of Notre Dame Press, 1984), p. 11, 12, 22.

10. Philip Rieff, *The Triumph of the Therapeutic: Uses of Faith after Freud* (Wilmington, DE: ISI Books, 2006), p. 4.

Chapter 6: Marxism, The Lie that Will Not Die

1. James Lindsay, *The Marxification of Education: Paulo Freire's Critical Marxism and the Theft of Education* (Orlando, FL: New Discourses), p. 33.

2. Noelle Mering, *Awake Not Woke: A Christian Response to the Cult of Progressive Ideology* (Gastonia, NC: TAN Books, 2021), p. 81.

3. C.S. Lewis, *The Screwtape Letters* (New York: HarperOne, 2001), p. 32.

4. Ibid., Preface, ix.

5. *The Bodies Others: The New Authoritarians, COVID-19 and The War Against the Human* (Fort Lauderdale, FL: All Seasons Press, 2022), p. 290, 291.

6. If you have any desire to learn more about Hegel and his thought, a good resource is found at this website of all things Marxist, https://www.marxists.org/reference/archive/hegel/index.htm

7. Paul Kengor, *The Devil and Karl Marx: Communism's Long March of Death, Deception, and Infiltration* (Gastonia, NC: TAN Books, 2020), p. 13.

8. https://www.marxists.org/archive/marx/works/1844/manuscripts/hegel.htm

9. Karl Marx & Frederick Engels, *The Communist Manifesto* (New York: International Publishers, 1948), p. 15.

10. https://www.thegospelcoalition.org/themelios/article/cultural-marxism-imaginary-conspiracy-or-revolutionary-reality/

11. Herbert Marcuse, *Reason & Revolution. Part II, The Rise of Social Theory*, published in 1941, from https://www.marxists.org/reference/archive/marcuse/works/reason/ch02-4.htm

12. Marx & Engels, Ibid., p. 9

13. Kengor, Ibid., p. 33.

14. Marx & Engels, Ibid., p. 5.

15. Ibid., p. 29.

16. Ibid., p. 23.

17. Ibid., p. 23.

18. Ibid., p. 26.

19. Ibid., p. 27.

20. Ibid., p. 27.

21. Ibid., p. 28.

22. Karl Marx, "A Contribution to the Critique of Hegel's Philosophy of Right," December 1843-January 1844, https://www.marxists.org /archive/marx/works/1843/critique-hpr/intro.htm

Chapter 7: The Birth of Cultural Marxism and Wokeness

1. Paul Kengor, *The Devil and Karl Marx: Communism's Long March of Death, Deception, and Infiltration* (Gastonia, NC: TAN Books, 2020), p. 347.

2. Ibid., p. 346.

3. Ibid., p. 147.

4. From *History and Class Consciousness*, p. 80. Quoted in James's Lindsay's *The Marxification of Education*. p. 95.

5. https://www.acton.org/religion-liberty/volume-29-number-3 /antonio-gramscis-long-march-through-history

6. I came across this quote from Trueman in a *Modern Reformation Magazine* article and saved it. I don't have the magazine so can't say what issue or article it appears in.

7. https://www.marcuse.org/herbert/publications/1960s/1965 -repressive-tolerance-fulltext.html

8. Dinesh D'Souza, *The Big Lie: Exposing the Nazi Roots of the American Left* (Washington, DC: Regnery), p. 211-214.

9. Ibid., p. 213.

10. I came across this literary exchange in a piece by Victor Davis Hanson titled, "Are Universities Doomed?" published in December 2022.

11. Noelle Mering, *Awake Not Woke: A Christian Response to the Cult of Progressive Ideology* (Gastonia, NC: TAN Books, 2021), p. 59.

12. Vivek Ramaswamy, *Woke, Inc. Inside Corporate America's Social Justice Scam* (New York: Center Street, 2021) p. 15.

13. Ibid., p. 135.

Chapter 8: How Marxism Infiltrated Education and the Classical Answer

1. Quoted in Alan Carlson, *The "American Way": Family and Community in the Shaping of the American Identity*, (Wilmington, DE: ISI Books, 2003), p. 6.

2. Rousas Rushdoony, *Intellectual Schizophrenia: Culture, Crisis and Education* (Philadelphia: Presbyterian and Reformed, 1961), p. 41.

3. J. Gresham Machen, *Education, Christianity and the State* (Unicoi, TN: The Trinity Foundation, 1987), p. 8, 9.

4. Ibid., p. 75.

5. Rushdoony, Ibid., p. 57.

6. Joseph Boot, *The Mission of God* (London: Wilberforce Publications, 2016), p. 450. Italics in the original.

7. Douglas Wilson, *The Case for Classical Christian Education* (Wheaton, IL: Crossway, 2003), p. 26.

8. Ibid., p. 54.

9. Ibid., p. 34.

10. I took these points from *Henry T. Edmondson III's John Dewey & The Decline of American Education* (Wilmington, DE: ISI Books), and the quote from p. 56.

11. Machen, Ibid., 14.

12. James Lindsay, *The Marxification of Education: Paulo Freire's Critical Marxism and the Theft of Education* (Orlando, FL: New Discourses, 2022). You can find more information at https://newdiscourses.com/

13. Ibid., p. xiv.

14. Ibid., p. 2.

15. Ibid., p. 1.

16. Ibid., p. 96.

17. Ibid., p. 96.

18. https://www.cfchildren.org/what-is-social-emotional-learning/

19. Ibid., p. 98.

20. Wilson, Ibid., 97.

Chapter 9: Progressivism, Progress and Globalist Tyranny

1. George Marsden, *Fundamentalism and American Culture*, Second Edition (New York: Oxford University Press, 2006), p. 15.

2. Ibid., p. 134.

3. Ibid., p. 51.

4. J.P. Moreland, *Scientism and Secularism: Learning to Respond to a Dangerous Ideology* (Wheaton, IL: Crossway, 2018), p. 26.

5. G.K. Chesterton, *The Three Apologies of G.K. Chesterton: Heretics, Orthodoxy & Everlasting Man* (Fairhope, AL: Mockingbird Press, 2018, Kindle Edition), p. 9.

6. C.S. Lewis, *God in the Dock* (Grand Rapids, MI: Eerdmans, 1970), p. 349, 350. Italics in original.

7. Herbert Schlossberg, *Idols for Destruction: Christian Faith and its Confrontation With American Society* (Nashville: Thomas Nelson, 1983), p. 231.

8. David Hackett Fischer, *Liberty and Freedom* (New York: Oxford University Press, 2005), p. 8.

9. Mark T. Mitchell, *Plutocratic Socialism: The Future of Private Property and the Fate of the Middle Class* (Eugene, OR: Front Porch Republic Books, 2022), p. 13.

Chapter 10: The Story of an Unlikely Christian Western Civilization

1. Thomas Cahill, *How the Irish Saved Civilization: The Untold Story of Ireland's Heroic Role from the Fall of Rome to the Rise of Medieval Europe* (New York: Anchor Books, 1995) p. 109-110.

2. Ibid., p. 3-4.

3. Winston S. Churchill, *A History of the English-Speaking Peoples: Volume 1, The Birth of Britain* (London: Bloomsbury Academic, 2015), p. 69.

4. Tom Holland, *Dominion: How the Christian Revolution Remade the World* (New York: Basic Books, 2019), p. 17.

5. Ibid., p. 406.

6. Churchill, Ibid., p. 69.

7. Ibid., p. 72.

8. Ryan Alford, *Seven Absolute Rights: Recovering the Historical Foundations of Canada's Rule of Law* (Montreal & Kingston: McGill-Queen's University Press, 2020), p. 80.

9. Churchill, Ibid., p. 155, 157.

10. Alford, Ibid., p. 85.

11. Ibid., p. 86

12. Yoram Hazony, *Conservatism: A Rediscovery* (Washington, DC: Regnery Gateway, 2022), p. 5.

13. Ibid., p. 13.

14. Alford, Ibid., p. 117.

Chapter 11: The Westphalian Nation-State and The Christian Nation

1. Stephen Wolfe, *The Case for Christian Nationalism* (Moscow, ID: Canon Press, 2022), p. 165.

2. Yoram Hazony, *Conservatism: A Rediscovery* (Washington, DC: Regnery Gateway, 2022), p. 397.

3. https://newsletters.theatlantic.com/the-third-rail/6377fb0d ce44df0038de4c62/respect-for-marriage-same-sex-religious-freedom/

4. Vishal Mangalwadi, *The Book that Made Your World: How the Bible Created the Soul of Western Civilization* (Nashville: Thomas Nelson, 2011), p. 138.

5. Abraham Kuyper, *Sphere Sovereignty* (from a public address delivered at the inauguration of the Free University of Amsterdam, Oct. 20, 1880).

6. Joseph Boot, *Ruler of Kings: Toward a Christian Vision of Government* (London: Wilberforce Publications, 2022), p. 144.

7. Wolfe, Ibid., p. 471.

8. Quoted in Joseph Boot, *The Mission of God* (London: Wilberforce Publications, 2016), p. 273.

9. Most well-meaning liberals who are not leftists will completely reject this, as will sadly most Christians. Both buy the theocracy is totalitarian charge to one degree or another, and think our only hope is some kind of non-religious (neutral) pluralistic state where on some pragmatic basis of potential societal harmony we can all just get along. As I've argued, neutrality is a myth.

10. Hazony, Ibid., p. 200.

11. Boot, Ibid., p. 274.

12. Boot, Ibid., p. 348, 350. Italics in the original.

13. Herbert Schlossberg, *Idols for Destruction: Christian Faith and its Confrontation with American Society* (Nashville: Thomas Nelson, 1983), p. 47.

14. Kuyper. Ibid.

15. Wolfe, Ibid., p. 247.

16. A discussion of natural law is well beyond the scope of this book, and is a terribly complicated topic because few people seem to agree on exactly what it is. The problem is that we now live in a post-Christian secular culture where biblical assumptions about the nature of reality are rejected, thus natural means "without God" to most people. In a Christian culture prior to the Enlightenment, the phrase would not have been problematic. Now I encourage Christians to replace the word natural with creation, as in creation law. Or we marvel not at nature, but at creation, and so on.

Chapter 12: The Founding of America

1. Patrick K. O'Donnell, *The Indispensables: The Diverse Soldier-Mariners who Shaped the Country, Formed the Navy, and Rowed Washington Across the Delaware* (New York: Atlantic Monthly Press, 2021), p. 53.

2. Ibid., p. 69.

3. Patrick K. O'Donnell, *Washington's Immortals: The Untold Story of an Elite Regiment Who Changed the Course of the Revolution* (New York: Grove Press, 2016), p. 39.

4. Ron Chernow, *Alexander Hamilton* (New York: The Penguin Press, 2004), p. 57.

5. Quote in *Mark David Hall, Proclaim Liberty Throughout the All the Land: How Christianity Has Advanced Freedom and Equality for All Americans* (Nashville: Fidelis Books, 2023), p. 65-66.

6. Timothy S. Goeglein, *Toward a More Perfect Union: The Moral and Cultural Care for Teaching the Great American Story.* (Nashville: Fidelis Books, 2023), p. 98.

7. Mark David Hall, *Did America Have a Christian Founding* (Nashville: Nelson Books, 2019), p. 2, a quote from their *Search for Christian America.*

8. https://amgreatness.com/2023/02/25/harry-jaffa-vs-willmoore -kendall-redivivus/

9. Sermon, "Dreams of a City on a Hill," 1630.

10. Robert Curry, *Common Sense Nation, Unlocking the Forgotten Power of the American Idea* (New York: Encounter Books, 2015), p. 135.

11. Russell Kirk, *Roots of American Order* (Wilmington, DE: ISI Books, 2003), p. 347.

12. Hazony, Ibid., p. 275.

13. Larry Schweikart and Michael Allen, *A Patriot's History of the United States: From Columbus's Great Discovery to America's Age of Entitlement* (New York: Sentinel, 2004), Introduction.

14. Curry., Ibid., p. 58.

15. Ibid., p. 62.

16. Ibid., p. 91.

17. Ibid., p. 92.

18. Douglas F. Kelly, *The Emergence of Liberty in the Modern World: The Influence of Calvin on Five Governments from the 16th through 18th Centuries* (Phillipsburg, NJ: P&R Publishing, 1992) p. 119.

NOTES TO PAGES 216-243

19. Mark A. Beliles and Stephen K. McDowell, *America's Providential History* (Charlottesville, VA: The Providence Foundation, 1989), Kindle version, Loc. 1769. Italics in the original.

20. Ibid., Loc. 3700.

Chapter 13: The Re-Founding of America

1. Eric Metaxas, *If You Can Keep It: The Forgotten Promise of American Liberty* (New York: Viking, 2016), p. 11.

2. Letter to General Philip Schuyler. On July 15, 1777, General St. Clair and his troops were defeated at Fort Ticonderoga. Schuyler informed Washington of the grave situations of his soldiers, but confirmed that the troops were not imprisoned by British forces. Washington responded assuring Schuyler this was not the end of the war.

3. "Encroaching Control," Ronald Reagan. On March 30, 1961, future governor and president Ronald Reagan gave a speech to the Phoenix Chamber of Commerce. No film remains of the event, only audio. It can be found on YouTube: https://www.youtube.com/watch?v=8gf9Y7UgGi0

4. George Washington statement to Gouverneur Morris prior to the start of the Constitutional Convention, May 1787.

5. https://www.powerlineblog.com/archives/2023/07/is-administra-tive-law-unlawful.php

6. https://www.firstthings.com/web-exclusives/2020/10/our-anti-catholic-administrative-state

7. R.R. Reno, *Return of the Strong Gods: Nationalism, Populism, and the Future of the West* (Washington, DC: Regnery Gateway, 2019), p. 40.

8. Ibid., p. 40.

9. Francis A. Schaeffer, *A Christian Manifesto* in *The Complete Works of Francis A. Schaeffer: A Christian Worldview* (Westchester, IL: Crossway Books, 1982), p. 423, 424. Italics in the original.

Chapter 14: Eschatology: The Theological Foundation for An Optimistic View of History, The Present, and the Future

1. Some people embrace what they call optimistic amillennialism, but I don't think you can pull that out of this eschatological position. I sure didn't.

2. Quoted in the preface to *A Postmillennial Primer: Basics of Optimistic Eschatology* by P. Andrew Sandlin.

3. From a lecture I heard on YouTube called "On the future of the world," and taken from his book, *Surprised by Hope*.

4. *Westminster Magazine*, Vol. 3, Issue 2, Spring 2023, "To the Ends of the Earth," by Stafford Carson.

5. *Lorraine Boettner, The Millennium, Revised Edition* (Phillipsburg, New Jersey: Presbyterian and Reformed Publishing Company, 1984), p. 60.

6. Ibid., p. 33.

7. https://subsplash.com/reformtheosem/learn-about-rts/mi/+kyyt246

8. P. Andrew Sandlin, *A Postmillennial Primer: Basics of Optimistic Eschatology* (Self Published, 2023), p. 39.

9. Greg L. Bahnsen, *Victory in Jesus: The Bright Hope of Postmillennialism* (Nacogdoches, TX: Covenant Media Press, 1999), p. 16, Italics in the original.

Concluding Post-Script

1. These ideas are taken from a talk by Joe Boot at a conference on postmillennialism in May 2023: Poisonous Pietism | Two Kingdoms Theology. https://www.youtube.com/watch?v=AFLrkEaP_Rw&t=18s

ABOUT THE AUTHOR

Mike D'Virgilio has a B.S. in Communication from Arizona State University and an M.A. in Systematic Theology from Westminster Theological Seminary Philadelphia. He has worked in public relations, sales, and marketing for over three decades. His first book was an exploration of apologetics for parents called, *The Persuasive Christian Parent: Building an Enduring Faith in You and Your Children.* He's also written a love letter in the form of a short book to his wife and children called, *Our Story: Mike & Sarah D'Virgilio's Excellent Adventure (Courtship)*, and his previous book was focused on the amazing verisimilitude in the Bible called, *Uninvented: How the Bible Could Not Be Made Up, and the Evidence that Proves It.* Amazon best selling author, he has also written for a variety of blogs over the years and currently writes on apologetics and a variety of topics at mikedvirgilio.com. His Twitter/X handle is @mdvirgilio, and Facebook @mike.dvirgilio.

ACKNOWLEDGMENTS

This book, like all my writing, was like standing on the shoulders of the giants who previously grappled with these big and important ideas. Its scope is massive, and there are multitudes of giants; I thank them all. Two of those who have been especially important in the development of my thinking while writing the book are Doug Wilson and Joe Boot. I must also give a special shoutout to Steven K. Bannon, who gets top billing in the book as the pivotal figure who changed my orientation from pessimism and defeatism to his gritty, realistic optimism. Closer to home, in it to be exact, I must thank my longsuffering wife, Sarah. I disappear into my home office for long periods of time to pursue my sales vocation, and my avocation, writing; she is always encouraging me. Her editing help was invaluable. Next to my wife, my greatest cheerleader is my best friend since 7th grade, Greg L. Smith, who reads everything I write and loves it, even when he shouldn't. Thanks also goes to Joanna and her team at Silversmith Press who helped me turn this into a product of which we can all be proud. And finally, and most importantly, to My Lord and Savior Jesus Christ who daily puts the puzzle pieces of my life together.

www.ingramcontent.com/pod-product-compliance
Lightning Source LLC
Chambersburg PA
CBHW050645270326
41927CB00012B/2878